The
COMPLETE TOMATO
Cookbook

The
COMPLETE TOMATO
Cookbook

by
Mable Hoffman

Illustrations by
Michelle Burchard

HPBooks

HPBooks
are published by
The Berkley Publishing Group
200 Madison Avenue
New York, NY 10016

Library of Congress Cataloging-in-Publication Data

Hoffman, Mable, 1922–
The complete tomato cookbook / Mable Hoffman :
illustrations by Michelle Burchard.
p.   cm.
Includes index.
ISBN 1-55788-097-2 (alk. paper)
1. Cookery (Tomatoes)   I. Title.
TX803.T6H64   1994
641.6′5642—dc20   94-3183
                                          CIP

Cover photograph © by D. Lada/H. Armstrong Roberts
Printed in the United States of America
1 2 3 4 5 6 7 8 9 10

NOTICE: The information printed in this book is true and complete
to the best of our knowledge. All recommendations
are made without any guarantees on the part of the author
or the publisher. The author and publisher disclaim
all liability in connection with the use of this information.

This book is printed on acid-free paper.
∞

Acknowledgments

I wish to thank Jan Robertson for her invaluable assistance in recipe testing and development, and thanks also to Grace Wheeler for her help.

Contents

Introduction

Spanish explorers are given credit for discovering tomatoes in the Americas. We are told that they returned to their country and introduced tomatoes without much success, because it was thought that tomatoes were poisonous. Eventually, both Spain and Italy accepted the product and became well known for their tomato dishes. Today most of us associate the Mediterranean area with tomato-based sauces and dishes. The tomato became popular in the United States in the late nineteenth century and is now widely accepted as an important part of our diet. Many of our best-known traditional recipes have been based on tomato products.

Botanically the tomato is a fruit, but for marketing purposes it is designated as a vegetable. The tomato is a rich source of vitamin C, beta-carotene, and potassium.

Today there are dozens of tomato varieties available. Each size and shape has its special role in the tomato world. The smallest or cherry tomato represents nature's individual miniature servings. They are handy for lunch boxes and picnics where they are eaten out-of-hand. Yellow and red pear tomatoes are used similarly to cherry tomatoes and are often added whole to salads. Larger tomatoes such as the globe tomatoes that are raised commercially and the beefsteak tomatoes are used for slicing, tossing with herbs, cheeses, and greens for salads, and for cooking into sauces or main dishes.

The entertainment industry revived an interest in fried green tomatoes with a movie by that name. Green tomatoes are firmer than ripe tomatoes, and ideal for frying or combining with other vegetables in relishes or salsas.

In recent years, sun-dried tomatoes have become the most talked-about tomato product. Although they seem rather expensive, the flavor is quite intense. Beautiful red tomatoes are dried, then packed dry in plastic bags or packed with olive oil in jars.

Although most of us prefer to buy fresh sun-ripened tomatoes at a neighborhood produce stand, or grow them in our backyard, there are many processed tomato products that enable us to enjoy tomatoes throughout the year. Over 75 percent of all tomatoes are used for processing. We have included a number of popular recipes featuring these products. In fact, several of our favorite recipes use a combination of fresh and processed tomatoes.

About Tomatoes

Tomato Terminology

Fresh Tomatoes

Sizes: Range from cherry tomatoes that are about one inch in diameter to very large varieties that measure about six inches across the center.

Shapes: Most tomatoes, both large and small, are round. Most commercial tomatoes are smooth, but other varieties often have ridges and crevices. A few varieties are pear-shaped; their texture is often more dense than that of their round cousins.

Colors: The basic color for tomatoes is red. We have added several recipes that feature green tomatoes. Their texture is firmer and their flavor is not as mellow as the riper, red ones. In addition tomatoes come in a variety of colors such as yellow, orange, white, pink, and striped combinations.

Processed Tomatoes & Tomato Products

Peeled and Diced Canned Tomatoes: Peeled and cut into small ready-to-use cubes in tomato juice; a versatile, time-saving tomato product.

Tomato Juice: Juice from fresh tomatoes, processed and available in bottles or cans.

Tomato Paste: Unseasoned, strained, concentrated tomatoes. It is so thick that it is almost a solid consistency. Most brands are without seasonings, but some include Italian herbs.

Tomato Puree: Unseasoned strained tomato pulp that has a consistency between tomato paste and tomato juice.

Tomato Sauce: Smooth tomato sauce with all-purpose seasonings. It is one of the most versatile tomato products. It is used in a wide variety of poultry, meat, fish, and cheese dishes.

Stewed Canned Tomatoes: Sliced or cut-up tomatoes, cooked with onions, celery, bell peppers, sugar, and spices.

Whole Canned Tomatoes: Peeled and packed in tomato juice without seasonings; may be sliced or chopped to suit the individual recipe.

Chili Sauce: Puree of tomatoes cooked to a thick consistency with sugar and vinegar. Similar to ketchup, except tomato seeds are not removed.

Green Chile Salsa: Jars of zesty ingredients including tomatoes, onions, and green chiles. Labeled according to degree of spiciness, from mild to hot.

Ketchup: Puree of tomatoes cooked to a thick consistency with sugar, vinegar, and spices. Flavors vary slightly, according to individual brands.

Marinara Sauce: An all-purpose sauce made of tomato puree, tomatoes, onions, olive oil, garlic, sugar, parsley, and other herbs. Handy as a quick pasta sauce or topping for pizza.

Picante Sauce: Exact ingredients vary according to individual brands. Most sauces include tomatoes, jalapeño chiles, green chiles, onions, bell peppers, cilantro, and spices. Several varieties are in refrigerated cases; other brands are shelf items. Look for labels that indicate intensity of heat.

Pizza Sauce: Combinations of tomato paste with seasonings that are compatible with pizzas; ready to serve.

Sun-dried Tomatoes

Tomatoes are dried either in the sun or in commercial dehydrators at low temperatures, resulting in a more intense flavor. They are usually packed as slices or halves in small plastic bags. Sometimes the dried tomatoes are chopped into tiny pieces and packed into jars to be added by the teaspoon to recipes. Store the tomatoes in a cool dry place and use within six months for the best flavor and color.

Sometimes dried tomato halves or slices are packed in oil after being dried. This variety is more pliable and resembles a roasted red pepper. Garlic and herbs are often added to sun-dried tomatoes that are packed in oil. After opening, the tomatoes packed in oil can be stored in the refrigerator for several months.

Both types of sun-dried tomatoes seem to be quite expensive, but they are used in small amounts in most recipes so they add a lot of flavor for a relatively small amount of money.

Popular Ways to Cut Fresh Tomatoes

To Slice

Choose medium-size or large firm tomatoes. With a sharp knife, make crosswise slices about three-eighths to one-half inch thick. A very popular addition to a variety of sandwiches, pizzas, or individual salad plates.

To Cut Wedges

Place a medium-size or large tomato, stem side down, on a cutting board. With a sharp knife, halve crosswise; then cut each half into three or four wedges. Attractive shapes for tossed salads or in pasta dishes.

To Make Tomato Cups

Cut off a thin slice across the top of each firm tomato. With a small spoon, scoop out the center seedy portion. If desired, make a notched edge on these cups by cutting small V-shaped wedges all around the top before they are filled. These make impressive containers for individual pasta salads or vegetable salads. They can also be stuffed with a meat or rice filling, then baked and served hot.

To Make Tomato Flowers

With the stem end down, make three or four equidistant cuts about two-thirds of the way through each tomato, being careful not to cut completely to the bottom. Very gently, spread each wedge out to form a space in the center. These make a delicious lunch when filled with chicken or tuna salad and served on a bed of greens.

TOMATO SIZES & YIELDS

When a recipe calls for a specific size of fresh tomato, you can count on these approximate weights and amounts.

SIZE	WEIGHT	CUPS WHEN CHOPPED
Cherry tomato	about 1 oz.	about 1 tablespoon
Plum tomato	2 to 3 oz.	about 1/3 cup
Small tomato	3 to 5 oz.	about 2/3 cup
Medium-size tomato	6 to 8 oz.	about 3/4 cups
Large tomato	8 to 12 oz.	about 1 1/4 cups
Extra-large tomato	12 to 16 oz.	about 2 cups

The COMPLETE TOMATO Cookbook

Appetizers

Everyone likes to sample small pieces of different foods, whether they are at a barbecue or an open house celebration. As a result, appetizers are so popular that it is difficult to determine how many to make for a party.

One answer to the problem is to make several kinds of appetizers and bring out a few of each at one time. Be sure everyone has had a chance to taste them. Then bring out more of the same ones, for those who are looking for seconds or thirds.

It helps to select dishes that can be made ahead of time. If possible, arrange the food on serving trays before the party, cover, and refrigerate until needed. For hot appetizers, keep them warm until serving time in an oven turned to very low.

Chile con Queso

This cheese and green chile dip is at its best when eaten soon after it is made.

2 tablespoons vegetable oil
1 small onion, chopped
2 tablespoons all-purpose flour
1 cup milk or half-and-half
2 medium-size tomatoes, peeled, seeded, and chopped
1 (4-oz.) can diced green chiles, drained
4 ounces Monterey Jack cheese, cubed (3/4 cup)
Tortilla chips

Heat oil in a 2-quart saucepan over medium heat. Add onion; sauté until softened. Add flour; cook, stirring, about 2 minutes. Reduce heat; gradually stir in milk. Cook, stirring, over low heat until thickened. Add tomatoes, chiles, and cheese. Cook, stirring, just until cheese begins to melt. Serve hot with chips. Makes 2 2/3 cups.

Pronto Dip

A hearty spicy sausage and cheese dip that can be put together in minutes.

1 (12-oz.) package bulk hot pork sausage
8 ounces sharp Cheddar cheese, shredded (2 cups)
2 small plum tomatoes, chopped
1 (4-oz.) can chopped green chiles or jalapeño chiles, drained
Corn chips or tortilla chips

Cook sausage in a medium-size skillet until browned, stirring to break up meat. Pour off fat. Reduce heat; add cheese, tomatoes, and chiles. Cook, stirring, over low heat until cheese begins to melt. Serve warm dip with corn chips. Makes about 3 cups.

Shortcut Bean Dip

A quick-and-easy appetizer to put together for unexpected guests, it uses ingredients you probably keep on hand.

1 (14- to 15-oz.) can pork and beans, drained
1 (4-oz.) can diced green chiles or jalapeño chiles, drained
1/4 cup sun-dried tomatoes in oil, drained
1 tablespoon prepared mustard
1 teaspoon prepared horseradish
2 tablespoons chopped green onions
1/4 cup shredded Cheddar cheese (1 oz.)
Corn chips or tortilla wedges

Finely chop beans, chiles, tomatoes, mustard, horseradish, green onions, and cheese in a blender or food processor. Pour puree into a medium-size saucepan; heat, stirring, until cheese melts. Serve warm as a dip with corn chips. Makes about 2 cups.

Variation

Canned navy beans can be substituted for the pork and beans. Drain and rinse before using.

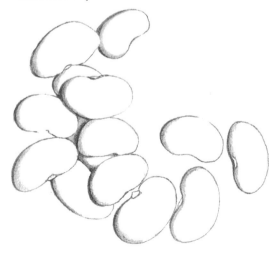

Sorrento Pickups

You can substitute one twelve-inch sourdough baguette for the two six-inch French rolls.
Use good-quality bread for the best flavor.

1/4 cup olive oil
1 garlic clove, crushed
2 unsliced large French rolls, about 6 inches long
2 tablespoons finely chopped Italian parsley
1/4 teaspoon finely chopped dried rosemary
1/4 cup finely chopped sun-dried tomatoes in oil, drained
1/2 cup crumbled goat cheese or shredded mozzarella cheese
Sliced ripe olives

Preheat broiler. Combine oil and garlic; set aside. Cut each roll into 1/2-inch crosswise slices. Place in a single layer on a large baking sheet. Brush tops with the garlic-flavored oil. Combine parsley, rosemary, and sun-dried tomatoes. Sprinkle on bread slices. Top with cheese. Broil 5 to 6 inches from source of heat about 2 minutes or until cheese begins to melt. Garnish each piece with sliced olives. Serve warm. Makes 24 appetizers.

Mediterranean Stuffed Mushrooms

The enticing flavors of herbs, sun-dried tomatoes, and pine nuts in the stuffing make a memorable impression.

24 medium-size mushrooms
2 tablespoons olive oil
1 small onion, coarsely chopped
1/2 teaspoon dried leaf oregano
1/4 teaspoon ground sage
1/4 teaspoon salt
1/8 teaspoon freshly ground pepper
1/2 cup sun-dried tomatoes in oil, drained and chopped
2 tablespoons chopped ripe olives
2 tablespoons coarsely chopped toasted pine nuts
2 tablespoons grated Parmesan cheese

Preheat oven to 350°F (175°C). Remove stems from mushrooms, reserving caps. Chop stems; reserve. Heat oil in a small skillet over medium heat. Add onion; cook until softened. Add mushroom stems; cook 1 minute, stirring occasionally. Stir in oregano, sage, salt, pepper, sun-dried tomatoes, olives, and nuts. Stuff into mushroom caps. Sprinkle with cheese. Place stuffed mushrooms on a baking sheet. Bake 6 to 8 minutes or until cheese melts. Makes 24 appetizers.

Three-Cheese Tomato Flan

This easy flan uses cracker crumbs to make the crust. The flavor is at its best when the flan is warm or at room temperature.

1 cup crushed sesame crackers (20 to 24 crackers)
3 tablespoons margarine or butter, melted
8 ounces ricotta cheese (1 cup)
4 ounces blue cheese, crumbled (2/3 cup)
3 ounces Neufchâtel cheese
2 eggs, slightly beaten
1/4 cup sun-dried tomatoes in oil, drained and chopped
Dairy sour cream (optional)
Chopped chives (optional)

Preheat oven to 350°F (175°C). Combine crackers and margarine in a small bowl. Press cracker mixture on bottom of a 9-inch quiche pan. Bake 8 to 10 minutes or until golden. Combine the cheeses in a medium-size bowl. Beat in eggs. Stir in sun-dried tomatoes. Carefully spoon over hot crust. Bake 25 to 30 minutes or until filling is set. Cool; cut into 16 to 18 thin wedges. Garnish each slice with a dab of sour cream and chives, if desired. Makes 16 to 18 servings.

Red Tomato Wings

These are a delicious finger food; serve with lots of colorful paper napkins.
Use the same sauce on drumsticks or thighs for a main dish.

12 chicken wings
1 (8-oz.) can tomato sauce
1/2 cup soy sauce
1/4 cup packed brown sugar
1 garlic clove, crushed
2 tablespoons vegetable oil

Cut wings into pieces at the joints; discard tip section. Place remaining wing pieces in a single layer in a 15 × 10-inch shallow baking pan. Combine tomato sauce, soy sauce, brown sugar, garlic, and oil in a small bowl. Pour sauce over chicken, cover, and refrigerate at least 2 hours. Preheat oven to 350°F (175°C). Bake, uncovered, 20 minutes. Turn and bake 20 to 25 minutes or until chicken is tender. Makes 24 appetizers.

Double-Cheese Cherry Tomatoes

A colorful addition to an appetizer tray. The filling can be made up to a day ahead;
fill tomatoes no more than two hours before serving.

25 to 30 cherry tomatoes
8 ounces cottage cheese (1 cup)
2 ounces blue cheese, crumbled (about 1/3 cup)
2 tablespoons mayonnaise
1 tablespoon prepared horseradish
1 teaspoon prepared mustard
2 teaspoons chopped chives
1/4 teaspoon salt
1/8 teaspoon freshly ground pepper

Cut a thin slice off tops of tomatoes; remove and discard seeds and pulp. Drain upside down on paper towels. Drain cottage cheese in a strainer about 15 minutes. Combine drained cottage cheese, blue cheese, mayonnaise, horseradish, mustard, chives, salt, and pepper in a medium-size bowl. Spoon about 2 teaspoons of cheese mixture into each tomato. Makes 25 to 30 appetizers.

Pita Pizza Wedges

A mini version of pizza that's quick to fix and easy to eat. This uses pita bread as the crust.

4 pita bread rounds
1 tablespoon olive oil
24 cherry tomatoes, quartered
12 slices pepperoni, cut into thin strips
1/2 cup green chile salsa, drained
4 ounces shredded mozzarella cheese (1 cup)

Preheat broiler. Arrange whole unsplit pita rounds on a baking sheet. Lightly toast under broiler. Brush pita tops with olive oil. Top each with cherry tomato wedges and pepperoni, then the salsa. Sprinkle tops with cheese. Broil about 1 minute or until cheese melts. Cut each round into 6 or 8 wedges. Makes 24 or 32 appetizers.

Layered Italian Pesto Squares

Ideal for a holiday get-together, these squares can be made the day before the party and kept refrigerated until serving time.

2 tablespoons fine dry bread crumbs
3 1/2 to 4 ounces thin sliced provolone cheese, halved (about 6 slices)
1 envelope unflavored gelatin
1/4 cup water
1 cup loosely packed basil leaves
1 garlic clove
1/4 cup olive oil
1/3 cup chopped sun-dried tomatoes
1/4 cup grated Parmesan cheese
1 cup tomato juice
1/3 cup dairy sour cream
1/4 cup chopped pistachios
Crackers or melba toast

Sprinkle bread crumbs over bottom of an 8-inch square pan. Layer provolone cheese slices over crumbs, slightly overlapping edges. Refrigerate while making pesto. Sprinkle gelatin over water in a 2-cup measure. Let stand 5 minutes to soften. Combine basil, garlic, and olive oil in a blender or food processor; process until finely chopped. Add sun-dried tomatoes and Parmesan cheese; process just to combine. Bring tomato juice to a boil in a small saucepan. Pour over softened gelatin; stir until dissolved. Add to basil mixture; process just to combine. Spoon over provolone cheese. Cover and refrigerate at least 2 hours or until firm. Spread sour cream over top; sprinkle with pistachios. Refrigerate until serving time. Cut into 1-inch squares. Serve each square on a cracker. Makes 50 to 60 squares.

Crabmeat & Brie Stuffed Peppers

A colorful and impressive way to start an important dinner party. The bell peppers can be roasted and filled up to four hours ahead; refrigerate until ready to broil. The tomato sauce can be made ahead, refrigerated, and heated just before serving.

3 large yellow bell peppers
2 tablespoons olive oil
1 leek, chopped
3 medium-size tomatoes, peeled, seeded, and chopped
1 (6-oz.) can tomato paste
1 tablespoon minced fresh basil
1 teaspoon chopped fresh oregano
1 garlic clove, crushed
1/2 teaspoon salt
1/8 teaspoon pepper
4 ounces crabmeat, flaked and picked over
1 (4-oz.) package Brie cheese, cut into 6 wedges
2 tablespoons slivered almonds

Preheat broiler or grill. Place whole bell peppers on a baking sheet and place under the broiler or on the grill rack. Broil or grill, turning several times, until skin is blistered and begins to turn black. Put peppers in a paper bag to cool about 15 minutes. Meanwhile, combine oil, leek, tomatoes, tomato paste, basil, oregano, garlic, salt, and pepper in a 2-quart saucepan. Bring to a boil; reduce heat and simmer 30 minutes. Remove roasted pepper from bag; peel off skin and remove stems. Halve each pepper lengthwise; discard seeds. Place equal amounts of crabmeat in bottom of each roasted pepper half. Top each with a wedge of brie; then with almonds. Place peppers on a baking sheet. Broil about 2 minutes or until cheese begins to melt. Spoon about 1/3 cup tomato sauce in center of each of six medium-size plates; top sauce with hot stuffed pepper halves. Makes 6 servings.

Pride-of-the-Garden Pâté

Make this two-toned vegetable pâté, then cover and refrigerate it several hours or overnight.

1 pound broccoli, coarsely chopped
1 medium-size onion, cut into 8 wedges
4 eggs
1/4 cup all-purpose flour
1/2 teaspoon salt
1/4 teaspoon freshly grated nutmeg
5 plum tomatoes, peeled, seeded, and chopped
1/2 cup seasoned dried bread crumbs
1 garlic clove, crushed
3/4 cup dairy sour cream
3/4 teaspoon dried dill weed
10 leaves curly endive

Preheat oven to 400°F (205°C). Grease an 8 × 4-inch loaf pan; set aside. Cook broccoli and onion in boiling water in a large saucepan about 12 minutes or until tender; drain. Process cooked broccoli and onion in a food processor or blender until pureed. Add 2 of the eggs, the flour, salt, and nutmeg. Pour into prepared pan; lightly press with back of spoon to make a level layer. Process tomatoes, remaining 2 eggs, bread crumbs, and garlic until finely chopped. Carefully spoon over broccoli layer. Cover pan with foil and set it in a 13 × 9-inch baking pan. Pour 8 or 9 cups of hot water around loaf pan. Bake 80 to 90 minutes or until pâté is firm. Remove pan from water bath. Refrigerate pâté in pan until chilled. Combine sour cream and dill in a small bowl. Cut chilled pâté into 10 (3/4-inch) slices. Line each serving plate with endive. Top with a slice of pâté, then a dab of dill sauce. Makes 10 servings.

Chilies, Soups, & Stews

Its flavor, texture, and colors make the tomato an ideal ingredient for these so-called comfort dishes. Soup is recognized as the dish to cure all ills.

Our collection has been updated to include some of the more contemporary chili dishes featuring today's popular ingredients such as black beans, goat cheese, and ground turkey. We have borrowed flavors from the Southwest to produce a Speedy Posole of yellow or white hominy, seasoned with tomatoes and accented with cilantro and green chiles.

With dried beans all the rage, we have included a variety of dishes that range from Sausage Bean Soup to a hearty Gringo Chili made with refried beans and topped with sour cream and tortilla chips.

Sausage Bean Soup

If you are hesitant about trying spicy foods, omit the hot pepper sauce
or start with a few drops and taste before adding more.

1 (12-oz.) package Portuguese or hot Italian sausage
2 ham hocks
1 medium-size onion, chopped
1 medium-size carrot, chopped
2 celery stalks, chopped
2 medium-size tomatoes, chopped
2 (8-oz.) cans tomato sauce
2 cups water
1/2 teaspoon salt
1/8 teaspoon freshly ground pepper
2 or 3 dashes hot pepper sauce
2 cups coarsely shredded cabbage
2 (16-oz.) cans dried lima beans, drained

Sauté sausage in a 4-quart pan about 5 minutes, stirring to break up meat. Drain off fat. Add ham hocks, onion, carrot, celery, tomatoes, tomato sauce, water, salt, pepper, and hot sauce. Cover and simmer 2 hours. Remove ham hocks; discard bone, skin, and fat. Cube meat and return to pot. Add cabbage and beans; cook about 30 minutes or until cabbage is tender. Makes 6 to 8 servings.

Hint-of-Tomato Squash Soup

This can be cooked and pureed ahead of time, then reheated just before serving.

2 or 3 pounds banana squash or butternut squash
2 (8-oz.) cans tomato sauce
1 (10 1/2-oz.) can condensed chicken broth
1/4 teaspoon ground coriander
1 garlic clove, crushed
1/2 teaspoon grated orange peel
1/2 teaspoon grated ginger root
1 teaspoon brown sugar
1/4 teaspoon salt
1/8 teaspoon freshly ground pepper
1/3 cup plain yogurt
1 tablespoon chopped chives

Peel, seed, and cut squash into 1/2-inch cubes. Combine in a large Dutch oven with tomato sauce, condensed broth, coriander, garlic, orange peel, ginger root, sugar, salt, and pepper. Cover; simmer about 40 minutes or until squash is very tender. Process in a food processor or blender until pureed. Reheat if needed. Top each serving with yogurt and chives. Makes 5 or 6 servings.

Italian Flavors Soup

A hearty soup that's produced in minutes, yet has traditional old-fashioned Italian flavors.

1 tablespoon vegetable oil
8 slices salami, cut into thin strips (about 1 1/2 oz.)
2 cups shredded cabbage
1 (8-oz.) can garbanzo beans, drained
1 (15- to 16-oz.) can diced peeled tomatoes in tomato juice
2 cups beef broth or bouillon
1/2 teaspoon dried Italian seasoning, crumbled
1/4 teaspoon salt
1/8 teaspoon freshly ground pepper

Heat oil in a 2-quart pan. Add salami; cook and stir over medium heat 2 or 3 minutes. Stir in cabbage, beans, tomatoes, broth, seasoning, salt, and pepper. Cover and simmer about 8 minutes or until cabbage is tender. Makes 4 or 5 servings.

Creamy Tomato Dill Soup

A refreshing cold tomato soup that's perfect as a first course at a summer dinner party.

1 tablespoon vegetable oil
1 onion, chopped
1 garlic clove, crushed
3 large tomatoes, peeled, seeded, and quartered
1 cup chicken broth or bouillon
3/4 teaspoon dried dill weed
1 teaspoon sugar
1/4 teaspoon salt
1/8 teaspoon freshly ground pepper
1 (12-oz.) can evaporated low-fat milk
1/4 cup dairy sour cream or plain low-fat yogurt

Heat oil in a 2-quart saucepan. Add onion and garlic; simmer 5 minutes or until onion is softened. Add tomatoes, broth, dill, sugar, salt, and pepper. Cover and simmer 20 minutes. Process in a blender or food processor until pureed; strain into a bowl. Stir in milk. Cover and refrigerate at least 2 hours. Pour into soup bowls; top with sour cream or yogurt. Makes 4 servings.

Fresh Cream of Tomato Soup

Tomatoes give this soup its fresh flavor and appetizing hue; the cream provides a smooth texture.

1 tablespoon vegetable oil
5 large tomatoes, peeled, seeded, and chopped
1 tablespoon chopped chives, plus additional as needed for garnish
1 tablespoon chopped fresh basil
1 tablespoon sugar
1/2 teaspoon salt
1/4 teaspoon seasoned salt
1/8 teaspoon freshly ground pepper
Pinch of freshly grated nutmeg
2 cups half-and-half

Heat oil in a 3-quart pan. Add tomatoes, chives, basil, sugar, salt, seasoned salt, pepper, and nutmeg. Simmer about 7 minutes. Process in a blender or food processor until pureed. Stir in half-and-half; heat to desired temperature without boiling. Sprinkle with additional chives. Makes 5 or 6 servings.

Turkey Stew & Rice

An ideal dish to prepare when you have roast turkey left from a big family dinner.

3 carrots, cut into 1/2-inch slices
1 (16-oz.) package frozen Italian-style green beans
2 leeks, cut into 1/2-inch slices
1 tablespoon finely chopped parsley
3 cups chicken broth or turkey broth
1 teaspoon curry powder
1/2 teaspoon salt

1/8 teaspoon freshly ground pepper
2 medium-size tomatoes, chopped
3 cups cubed cooked turkey
1 cup long-grain white rice

Combine carrots, beans, leeks, parsley, broth, curry powder, salt, and pepper in a large saucepan. Cover and simmer about 15 minutes or until carrots are almost tender. Add tomatoes and cooked turkey. Cook another 5 minutes. Meanwhile, cook rice according to package directions. Spoon into large individual soup bowls; cover with turkey stew. Makes about 6 servings.

Farm-Style Corn Chowder

A hearty chowder that is filling enough to be used as a main dish.

1 onion, finely chopped
6 to 8 ounces smoky sausage links, sliced
1 potato, finely chopped
2 cups chicken broth or bouillon
1 (16-oz.) can cream-style corn
1/4 cup canned diced green chiles
2 medium-size tomatoes, chopped
1/4 teaspoon salt
1/4 teaspoon garlic salt

Combine onion, sausage, potato, and broth in a 2-quart saucepan. Cover and simmer over low heat 15 minutes. Stir in corn, chiles, tomatoes, salt, and garlic salt. Cover; simmer 4 or 5 minutes. Makes about 6 servings.

Short Rib Stew

Choose extra-lean short ribs; if they are not available, carefully brown the ribs on all sides and pour off the grease before adding other ingredients.

2 1/2 to 3 pounds lean short ribs
2 leeks, cut into 1/2-inch slices
4 carrots, cut into 1/2-inch pieces
4 new potatoes, quartered
4 plum tomatoes, quartered
1/2 teaspoon dried leaf marjoram
1 teaspoon Worcestershire sauce
1/2 teaspoon salt
1/8 teaspoon freshly ground pepper
2 cups beef broth or bouillon
1/4 cup cornstarch
1/4 cup cold water

Heat a large Dutch oven over medium heat. Add short ribs; brown on all sides. Pour off grease. Add leeks, carrots, potatoes, tomatoes, marjoram, Worcestershire sauce, salt, pepper, and broth. Cook, covered, 2 hours or until tender. Dissolve cornstarch in the cold water; stir into hot stew. Cook over low heat, stirring constantly, until thickened. Makes 5 or 6 servings.

Speedy Posole

Large soup bowls are ideal for serving this dish because it has quite a bit of wonderful broth, yet is much heartier than most soups.

1 pound lean boneless pork, cut into 1/2-inch cubes
1 (4-oz.) can diced green chiles, drained
1 small onion, chopped
1 (15- or 16-oz.) can diced peeled tomatoes in tomato juice
1 garlic clove, crushed
1 teaspoon chili powder
1/2 teaspoon salt
2 cups chicken broth or bouillon
1 (29-oz.) can white or yellow hominy, drained
1 tablespoon chopped cilantro
1/4 cup dairy sour cream or plain yogurt

Combine pork cubes, green chiles, onion, tomatoes, garlic, chili powder, salt, broth, and hominy in a 4-quart pan. Cover and simmer 30 to 35 minutes or until meat is tender. Add cilantro; spoon into large individual soup bowls. Top each bowl with sour cream or yogurt. Makes about 6 servings.

Black Bean Chili with Goat Cheese

Puree one can of the beans and use the other one as is for a slightly thickened soup with lots of texture.

1 tablespoon vegetable or olive oil
1 medium-size onion, chopped
1 yellow or green bell pepper, chopped
1 garlic clove, crushed
1 jalapeño chile, seeded and chopped
1 (28-oz.) can chopped peeled tomatoes
1 teaspoon chili powder
1/2 teaspoon paprika
1/2 teaspoon salt
1/2 teaspoon dried leaf oregano
2 (15- or 16-oz.) cans black beans
4 or 5 ounces crumbled goat cheese

Heat oil in a 3- or 4-quart pan. Add onion, bell pepper, garlic, and chile. Cook until onion is softened. Add tomatoes, chili powder, paprika, salt, and oregano. Process 1 can of beans in a blender or food processor until pureed. Drain remaining can of beans. Add pureed beans and drained whole beans to tomato mixture. Cover; simmer 5 to 10 minutes. Serve in large individual soup bowls. Sprinkle each serving with goat cheese. Makes 6 to 8 servings.

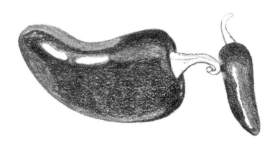

Green Chile Stew

Choose one or all the toppings to highlight this hearty, spicy stew.

2 tablespoons vegetable oil
1 pound boneless pork, cut into 1/2-inch cubes
2 cups (1/2-inch cubes) potatoes
1 large onion, chopped
2 garlic cloves, crushed
1 cup green tomatillo salsa
1 (14 1/2-oz.) can diced tomatoes in tomato juice
1 (7-oz.) can diced green chiles
Sour cream, shredded Monterey Jack cheese, and chopped fresh cilantro leaves

Heat oil in a large saucepan over medium heat. Add pork and cook until lightly browned. Add potatoes, onion, garlic, salsa, tomatoes, and chiles. Bring to a boil. Reduce heat; cover, and simmer 25 minutes or until meat and potatoes are tender, stirring several times. Pass small bowls of sour cream, shredded cheese, and chopped cilantro for toppings. Makes 5 or 6 servings.

Pinto Turkey Chili

Picante sauce plus chili powder provides a spicy flavor combination.

1 tablespoon vegetable oil
1 pound ground turkey
1 (28-oz.) can diced peeled tomatoes in tomato juice
1 cup bottled picante sauce
1 medium-size onion, chopped
2 medium-size zucchini, coarsely shredded
1 (15- to 16-oz.) can pinto beans, drained
1 tablespoon chili powder
1/4 teaspoon cumin
1/2 teaspoon salt

Heat oil in a 3-quart saucepan over medium heat. Add ground turkey; cook until no longer pink, stirring to break up meat. Add tomatoes, picante sauce, onion, zucchini, pinto beans, chili powder, cumin, and salt. Simmer, covered, 40 to 45 minutes or until onion is done. Makes 6 to 8 servings.

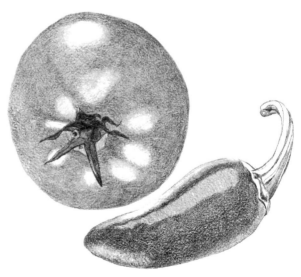

Gringo Chili

Increase or decrease the amount of chili powder and jalapeño chile according to your family's taste.

1 (12-oz.) package hot pork sausage
1 yellow bell pepper, chopped
3 medium-size tomatoes, chopped
2 green onions, sliced
1 cup chicken broth or bouillon
1 garlic clove, crushed
2 teaspoons chili powder
1 jalapeño chile, seeded and finely chopped
1/2 teaspoon salt
1 (15- to 16-oz.) can refried beans
1/3 cup dairy sour cream or plain yogurt
1 cup crushed corn chips or tortilla chips
1 tablespoon chopped cilantro

Cook sausage in a 3-quart saucepan over medium heat until lightly browned, stirring to break up meat. Drain off fat. Add bell pepper, tomatoes, green onions, broth, garlic, chili powder, jalapeño chile, and salt. Simmer, covered, 25 to 30 minutes. Stir in refried beans; heat until bubbly, stirring frequently. Spoon into large individual bowls. Top with sour cream and corn chips. Sprinkle with cilantro. Makes 5 or 6 servings.

Tomato Beef Bouillon

As a first course, serve it with thin lemon slices. For a heartier version, offer a choice of toppings.

1 (46-oz.) can tomato juice
1 (10 1/2-oz.) can condensed beef broth
2 small bay leaves
1/4 teaspoon ground thyme
1/8 to 1/4 teaspoon freshly ground pepper
1/8 teaspoon ground cloves
3/4 cup dry sherry
1 lemon, thinly sliced

Combine tomato juice and beef broth in a large saucepan. Add bay leaves, thyme, pepper, and cloves. Bring mixture to a boil. Reduce heat, cover, and simmer 15 minutes. Remove and discard bay leaves. Stir in sherry. Serve in mugs or bowls with a thin lemon slice floating on top of each. Makes 6 to 8 servings.

Variation

Offer toppings of shredded Cheddar cheese, bay shrimp, miniature meatballs, croutons, thinly sliced green onion or chopped parsley, coarsely ground pepper, and whipped butter.

Portuguese Red Bean Soup

Make a complete meal with this hearty and flavorful soup.

8 ounces smoked sausage, cut into 1/4-inch slices
1 (15 1/2-oz.) can small red beans, undrained
1 (14 1/2-oz.) can diced tomatoes with tomato juice
3 cups water
1 small onion, chopped
1 medium-size potato, diced
3 medium-size garlic cloves, thinly sliced crosswise
1 teaspoon paprika
1/2 teaspoon salt or to taste
1/4 teaspoon freshly ground black pepper
1/8 teaspoon ground red (cayenne) pepper
2 cups lightly packed chopped green cabbage
1/4 cup small elbow macaroni
1 tablespoon lemon juice

Put sausage into a large saucepan. Add beans, tomatoes, water, onion, potato, garlic, paprika, salt, black pepper, and cayenne. Bring to a boil. Reduce heat, cover, and simmer 10 to 15 minutes or until potatoes are almost tender. Stir in cabbage, macaroni, and lemon juice. Cook, uncovered, 15 to 20 minutes or until potatoes and macaroni are tender, stirring occasionally. Makes 4 to 6 servings.

Mediterranean Fish Stew

Serve with crusty Italian or French bread and a tossed green salad.

2 tablespoons extra-virgin olive oil
1 small onion, finely chopped
4 large tomatoes, peeled, seeded, and chopped
1 (8-oz.) can tomato sauce
1/2 pound red potatoes, cut into 1/2-inch cubes
1 (8-oz.) bottle clam juice
1/4 cup dry white wine
1 large garlic clove, minced
1/2 teaspoon fennel seeds, crushed
1/2 teaspoon dried leaf thyme, crushed
1/2 teaspoon dried leaf basil, crushed
1 large bay leaf
1/2 teaspoon salt
1/8 teaspoon freshly ground pepper
1 1/2 pounds boneless firm fish, cut into 1-inch chunks
1/3 cup chopped fresh parsley

Heat oil in a 2-quart saucepan or Dutch oven over medium heat. Add onion; sauté until softened. Add tomatoes, tomato sauce, potatoes, clam juice, wine, garlic, fennel seeds, thyme, basil, bay leaf, salt, and pepper. Bring to a boil. Reduce heat, cover, and simmer 15 to 20 minutes. Remove bay leaf and discard. Add fish; simmer 12 to 15 minutes or until fish turns from translucent to opaque. Stir in parsley. Makes 5 or 6 servings.

Southwestern Cheese Soup

Blue-corn tortilla chips are an ideal accompaniment to this rich, hearty soup.

2 tablespoons margarine or butter
1 small onion, chopped
1 cup chopped celery
3 large tomatoes, peeled, seeded, and chopped
2 small potatoes (about 1/2 pound), cut into 1/2-inch cubes
1 small garlic clove, crushed
1 teaspoon ground cumin
1 teaspoon fresh oregano, finely chopped
1/2 teaspoon salt
3 tablespoons all-purpose flour
1 cup milk
2 cups half-and-half
1/4 cup dry white wine
8 ounces pepper Jack cheese, shredded (2 cups)

Melt margarine in a 2-quart saucepan. Add onion and celery. Cook until onion is softened. Stir in tomatoes, potatoes, garlic, cumin, oregano, and salt. Cook until potatoes are tender. Whisk together flour and milk. Remove soup from heat. Add flour mixture, stirring to mix. Return to heat. Stir in half-and-half; cook, stirring constantly, until slightly thickened. Add wine. Remove from heat; gradually stir in cheese. Keep warm over low heat but do not allow to boil. Makes 5 or 6 servings.

Main Dishes

Tomato-based main dishes vary from nostalgic choices such as Favorite Barbecued Spareribs to Grilled Chicken with Confetti Salsa. There are casseroles and skillet dishes designed to make it easy for you to prepare a delicious meal with very little effort. Some are classics, while others use today's updated techniques and ingredients to produce new and exciting combinations.

All of them rely on a fresh or processed tomato product to provide flavor and appetite appeal. Then we have added compatible spices and herbs to bring out the best in the tomatoes.

When you know you are going to be pressed for time, make up a casserole-type dish and refrigerate before you leave for work or errands, then bake it at dinner time.

Speedy Sausage Dinner

Colorful yet tasty combination to serve when the family is clamoring for dinner and you are running late. Heat a loaf of French bread and toss a green salad while this simmers, and get some help with setting the table and you can have dinner in thirty minutes.

6 to 8 ounces smoky sausage links
1 (11-oz.) can Mexi-corn, undrained, or 1 (8 1/4-oz.) jar baby corn, drained
2 zucchini, thinly sliced
2 medium-size tomatoes, diced
1 garlic clove, crushed
1/2 teaspoon chili powder
1/4 teaspoon salt
1/8 teaspoon freshly ground pepper

Cut sausage into 1/2-inch slices. Heat in a 10-inch skillet. Stir in corn, zucchini, tomatoes, garlic, chili powder, salt, and pepper. Simmer 10 to 15 minutes, stirring occasionally. Makes 4 or 5 servings.

Curried Pork & Rice

A sprinkle of chopped peanuts and a bit of chutney provide the finishing touches to this easy skillet dish.

1 tablespoon vegetable oil
5 or 6 boneless pork chops or cutlets
1 cup long-grain white rice
2 medium-size tomatoes, peeled and diced
1 small onion, chopped
1 garlic clove, crushed
2 cups chicken broth

1 teaspoon curry powder
1/2 teaspoon salt
1/8 teaspoon freshly ground pepper

Heat oil in a 10-inch skillet. Add pork chops; cook until lightly browned. Add uncooked rice, tomatoes, onion, garlic, broth, curry powder, salt, and pepper. Cover and simmer 35 to 45 minutes or until chops are tender and most of the liquid has been absorbed. Makes 5 or 6 servings.

Variation

Chicken pieces can be substituted for the pork. Simmer about 30 minutes.

Chicken & Rice Skillet

A skillet dish that incorporates so many popular flavors that it will become one of your favorites.

3 bacon slices, chopped
6 chicken thighs or chicken breast halves
1 cup long-grain rice
1 onion, cut into 6 wedges
1 yellow or green bell pepper, sliced
3 medium-size tomatoes, chopped
1/2 teaspoon salt
1/8 teaspoon freshly ground black pepper
1 cup chicken broth
1 tablespoon chopped parsley

Cook bacon in a 12-inch skillet until almost crisp. Drain off some fat, if desired. Add chicken; cook until lightly browned. Stir in uncooked rice, onion, bell pepper, tomatoes, salt, black pepper, and broth. Cover and simmer 30 to 40 minutes or until chicken is tender. Sprinkle parsley over top. Makes 6 servings.

Pronto Malaysian Chicken

Put dinner on the table within minutes with this interesting chicken dish with a foreign accent.

6 boneless skinless chicken breast halves
1 tablespoon lime juice or lemon juice
1 teaspoon chili powder
2 tablespoons vegetable oil
1 medium-size onion, thinly sliced
1 mild green chile, chopped
2 medium-size tomatoes, chopped
1/2 teaspoon salt
1 teaspoon grated ginger root
1/4 teaspoon turmeric
1 tablespoon honey
Cooked rice or noodles

Cut chicken into bite-size pieces. Sprinkle with lime juice, then with chili powder. Heat oil in a 10-inch skillet. Add chicken; cook, stirring occasionally, until lightly browned on all sides. Stir in onion, chile, tomatoes, salt, ginger root, turmeric, and honey. Cover and simmer about 10 minutes or until chicken is done. Spoon over cooked rice or noodles. Makes 6 servings.

Grilled Chicken with Confetti Salsa

Substitute a jalapeño chile for the green chile if you like more heat in your salsa.

8 chicken thighs or breasts
2 tablespoons vegetable oil
1/2 teaspoon salt
1/8 teaspoon freshly ground pepper

Confetti Salsa:

2 cups cherry tomatoes, quartered (1 pint basket)
1/2 cup chopped peeled jicama
1 ear corn, cooked and cut off the cob (about 1 cup)
2 tablespoons chopped cilantro
1 small mild green chile, chopped
1 green onion, finely chopped
1 tablespoon vegetable oil
1/4 teaspoon seasoned salt

Preheat grill or broiler. Prepare salsa, cover, and refrigerate. Brush chicken with vegetable oil; sprinkle with salt and pepper. Grill or broil 5 inches from source of heat about 5 minutes. Turn; brush with oil. Grill another 3 to 4 minutes or until juices run clear when chicken is cut. Serve warm with salsa. Makes 8 servings.

Confetti Salsa:

Combine all ingredients in a medium-size bowl.

Skillet Sunday Brunch

Assemble everyone before you put the eggs on, because this dish is at its very best as soon as it is done.

1 tablespoon olive oil or vegetable oil
3 ounces prosciutto, cut into small strips (about 1/2 cup)
1 small onion, chopped
5 large tomatoes, peeled, seeded, and chopped
3 or 4 large mushrooms, diced
1 tablespoon chopped fresh basil
1/4 teaspoon salt
1/8 teaspoon freshly ground pepper
1 teaspoon Worcestershire sauce
4 or 5 eggs
2 tablespoons grated Parmesan cheese
4 or 5 English muffin halves

Heat oil in a large skillet. Add prosciutto and onion; cook over low heat until onion is softened. Stir in tomatoes, mushrooms, basil, salt, pepper, and Worcestershire sauce. Cook, uncovered, over medium heat about 15 minutes or until slightly thickened, stirring occasionally. With back of a wooden spoon, make 4 or 5 indentations in top of tomato mixture. Drop one uncooked egg into each. Sprinkle top with cheese. Cover and cook over medium-low heat about 5 minutes or until eggs are desired doneness. Toast English muffins. Carefully spoon a cooked egg on each muffin half. Spoon remaining sauce over all. Makes 4 or 5 servings.

Honey-Mustard Baked Chicken

Just a hint of honey and mustard flavors the marinade.

1 (6-oz.) can tomato paste
2 tablespoons Dijon mustard
1/2 cup plain low-fat yogurt
2 tablespoons honey
1/4 teaspoon salt
1/8 teaspoon freshly ground pepper
1 (3- to 3 1/2-lb.) chicken, cut up

Combine tomato paste, mustard, yogurt, honey, salt, and pepper in a small bowl. Pour over chicken, cover, and refrigerate at least 2 hours. Preheat oven to 375°F (190°C). Arrange chicken in a single layer with marinade in a 13 × 9-inch baking dish. Bake, uncovered, about 50 minutes or until tender. Makes 5 or 6 servings.

Tip

A self-sealing plastic bag is perfect for marinating the chicken pieces. The chicken can be turned in the marinade without opening the bag.

Sausage-Macaroni Quiche

A surprisingly easy, delicious main dish to feature at your next Sunday brunch.
Serve with a fresh fruit salad.

8 ounces small macaroni or small shells (about 2 cups uncooked)
3 eggs, slightly beaten
2 cups milk
4 ounces smoked sausage links, cut into bite-size pieces
2 green onions, chopped
1/4 teaspoon salt
1/8 teaspoon freshly ground pepper
2 tomatoes, peeled and sliced
8 ounces shredded Cheddar cheese (2 cups)
1/4 cup seasoned dried bread crumbs

Cook pasta according to package directions; drain and set aside. Preheat oven to 325°F (165°C). Grease an 11-inch ceramic quiche pan or a 13 × 9-inch baking dish. While pasta cooks, combine slightly beaten eggs, milk, sausage, green onions, salt, and pepper in a large bowl. Arrange cooked pasta in the bottom of greased dish. Spoon egg mixture over cooked pasta. Arrange tomatoes on top. Toss cheese with bread crumbs. Sprinkle over top. Bake, uncovered, 45 to 55 minutes or until firm. Cut into 6 to 8 wedges or rectangles.

Turkey Burger Cheese Pie

One of our favorite individual casseroles with an easy golden biscuit topping.

12 ounces uncooked ground turkey
1/2 teaspoon salt
1/8 teaspoon freshly ground pepper
1/2 teaspoon chili powder
2 medium-size tomatoes, sliced
4 ounces shredded Cheddar cheese (1 cup)
1 cup light sour cream
1/2 cup light mayonnaise
1 tablespoon chopped green onions
2/3 cup milk
1 egg, slightly beaten
1 1/2 cups baking mix

Cook ground turkey in a 10-inch skillet until lightly browned, stirring to break up meat. Add salt, pepper, and chili powder. Preheat oven to 375°F (190°C). Spoon turkey into bottom of eight 4 1/2-inch individual tart pans. Top with tomato slices. Combine cheese, sour cream, mayonnaise, and onions in a small bowl. Spoon over tomatoes. Process milk, egg, and baking mix until smooth in a food processor or mix in a small bowl to form a soft dough. Spoon equal amounts on top of each pie. Bake 18 to 20 minutes or until golden brown. Makes 8 servings.

Variation

Add 1 teaspoon dried leaf oregano and 1/2 teaspoon coarsely ground pepper to the baking mix before adding milk and egg.

Cacciatore-style Chicken Breasts

A dish of cooked pasta provides a perfect base for this flavorful chicken.

3 tablespoons olive oil
6 (4-oz.) boneless skinless chicken breast halves
1 medium-size onion, cut in half lengthwise and thinly sliced
1 medium-size green bell pepper, slivered
1 cup sliced fresh mushrooms
2 medium-size garlic cloves, minced
1 (14 1/2-oz.) can diced tomatoes with tomato juice
3 tablespoons tomato paste
1/2 cup dry white wine
1 teaspoon dried leaf basil, crushed
1/2 teaspoon dried leaf oregano, crushed
1/2 teaspoon dried leaf thyme, crushed
1 large bay leaf
1/2 teaspoon salt
1/4 teaspoon freshly ground black pepper
1/4 cup chopped Italian parsley
Cooked spaghetti or linguine

Heat olive oil in a large heavy skillet or Dutch oven over medium heat. Add chicken; brown about 2 minutes on each side. Remove from pan and set aside. Add onion, bell pepper, mushrooms, and garlic; sauté until onion is lightly browned, 3 or 4 minutes. Combine tomatoes, tomato paste, wine, basil, oregano, thyme, bay leaf, salt, and black pepper in a medium-size bowl. Return chicken and juices to pan. Add tomato mixture. Cover and simmer 15 minutes. Stir and cook, uncovered, 10 to 15 minutes or until chicken is tender. Remove and discard bay leaf. Add parsley. Serve over cooked pasta. Makes 6 servings.

Pizza Meat Round

Use a pan with a solid bottom; juices will leak out of a pan with a removable bottom.
Toss some potato wedges in olive oil and bake in the same oven with the meat.

1 pound lean ground beef
1/2 cup fine dried bread crumbs
1 small onion, finely chopped
1/2 cup chopped fresh or canned mushrooms
1/2 teaspoon salt
1/8 teaspoon freshly ground pepper
1 egg, slightly beaten
1/2 teaspoon dried leaf oregano
1/4 teaspoon dried leaf basil
1 teaspoon Worcestershire sauce
1 (8-oz.) can tomato sauce
2 ounces shredded mozzarella cheese (1/2 cup)

Preheat oven to 350°F (175°C). Combine ground beef, bread crumbs, onion, mushrooms, salt, pepper, egg, oregano, basil, and Worcestershire sauce in a medium-size bowl. Stir in half the tomato sauce. Pat into bottom of a round 9-inch baking pan. Top with remaining tomato sauce. Bake about 45 minutes or until meat is firm. Remove from oven; immediately sprinkle with cheese. Cut into wedges. Makes 5 or 6 servings.

Favorite Barbecued Spareribs

These ribs can be finished on the grill or under the broiler. Simmering the ribs until tender makes them juicier. The barbecue sauce will burn during grilling if the fire is too hot or the ribs are too close to the heat source.

3 1/2 to 4 pounds pork spareribs, cut into 2 or 3 rib sections
1 cup ketchup
2 tablespoons vinegar
1 tablespoon brown sugar
1 tablespoon dry mustard
1 tablespoon Worcestershire sauce
1 tablespoon honey
1/2 teaspoon chili powder
1/2 teaspoon salt
2 or 3 drops hot pepper sauce (optional)

Cover ribs with water in a large pot. Simmer 35 to 40 minutes or until tender. To make sauce, combine ketchup, vinegar, brown sugar, mustard, Worcestershire sauce, honey, chili powder, salt, and hot pepper sauce, if using, in a medium-size saucepan. Cook, stirring, over medium heat until bubbly. Preheat grill or broiler. Drain ribs; cover both sides of ribs with barbecue sauce. Broil or grill about 4 inches from source of heat about 5 minutes. Turn and broil other side about 5 minutes or until browned. Makes 4 or 5 servings.

New World Cabbage Rolls

*A delightful blend of spices with rice and meat, encased in cabbage leaves,
then topped with a purchased marinara sauce.*

1 large cabbage head
1 pound lean ground beef or lamb
1 small onion, chopped
1 egg, slightly beaten
1 cup cooked rice
1/2 teaspoon dried Italian seasoning
1 teaspoon Worcestershire sauce
1/2 teaspoon salt
1/8 teaspoon freshly ground pepper
1 (16-oz.) jar marinara sauce

Carefully remove 12 large cabbage leaves from head. Drop leaves into a large pan of boiling water. Simmer about 3 minutes or until leaves are limp; rinse in cold water. Drain and set aside. Combine meat, onion, egg, rice, seasoning, Worcestershire sauce, salt, and pepper in a medium-size bowl. Spoon about 1/4 cup meat mixture in center of each blanched leaf. Fold in sides and roll ends over filling. Place, seam side down, in a 10-inch skillet. Pour sauce over cabbage rolls. Cover; simmer 35 to 40 minutes or until cabbage is tender and meat is cooked. Makes 12 rolls.

Variation

Substitute two recipes Home-style Tomato Sauce (page 113) or one recipe Marinara Sauce with Fresh Herbs (page 118) for the jar of marinara sauce.

Hungarian Goulash

A hearty main dish that you can make ahead, then reheat at serving time.

1/3 cup all-purpose flour
1 teaspoon caraway seeds
1 teaspoon salt
1/2 teaspoon freshly ground pepper
1 1/2 pounds boneless beef round steak, cut into 3/4-inch cubes
1 tablespoon vegetable oil
1 large onion, chopped
1 tablespoon sweet Hungarian paprika
1 (28-oz.) can diced tomatoes with tomato juice
1 tablespoon tomato paste
1/4 cup dry red wine
2 small garlic cloves, crushed
Buttered noodles or spaetzle

Preheat oven to 325°F (165°C). Combine flour, caraway seeds, salt, and pepper in a bowl or plastic bag. Toss beef cubes in flour mixture. Heat oil in a 2-quart Dutch oven. Add meat and cook until browned. Add onion; cook until translucent. Stir in paprika and any remaining flour mixture. Add tomatoes with juice, tomato paste, wine, and garlic. Bake, covered, 1 1/2 to 2 hours or until beef is tender, stirring after 1 hour. Serve over cooked buttered noodles or spaetzle. Makes 5 or 6 servings.

Broiled Fish Tacos

Here is a popular taco that is low in fat and filled with good-tasting healthful ingredients.
Often the fish in fish tacos is deep-fried, but here it is broiled.

8 (about 6-inch-diameter) corn tortillas
1 pound fish fillets, about 1 inch thick
1 tablespoon vegetable oil
1/4 teaspoon seasoned salt
1/8 teaspoon freshly ground pepper
2 cups shredded cabbage
2 medium-size tomatoes, chopped
1 small onion, chopped
1 small jicama, peeled and coarsely shredded (about 1 cup)
2 tablespoons chopped cilantro
1/2 cup prepared taco sauce
Dairy sour cream (optional)

Preheat oven to 400°F (205°C). Wrap tortillas in foil. Heat in oven about 10 minutes or until warm. Preheat broiler. Brush top of fish with half the oil; sprinkle with salt and pepper. Broil 4 to 5 inches from heat source 5 minutes. Turn fish, brush with oil, and broil about 4 minutes or until fish just begins to flake when tested with a fork. Combine cabbage, tomatoes, onion, jicama, cilantro, and taco sauce in a medium-size bowl. Cut fish into bite-size pieces. Place about 1/3 cup cooked fish on each warm tortilla. Spoon cabbage mixture over fish. Top with sour cream, if using. Makes 8 tacos.

Tomato-baked Swordfish Steaks

The foil covering keeps this colorful fish dish moist and delicious.

2 medium-size tomatoes, peeled, seeded, and chopped
2 green onions, chopped
1 yellow or red bell pepper, julienned
1/2 teaspoon salt
1/8 teaspoon freshly ground black pepper
6 swordfish steaks, about 1 inch thick

Preheat oven to 350°F (175°C). Combine tomatoes, green onions, bell pepper, salt, and black pepper in a medium-size bowl. Arrange fish in a 13 × 9-inch baking dish. Spoon tomato mixture over fish. Cover with foil. Bake about 35 minutes or until fish just begins to flake when tested with a fork. Makes 6 servings.

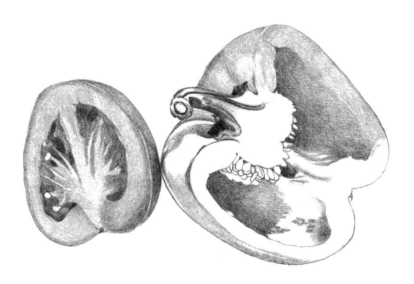

Fisherman's Special

Purchasing the sauce makes this fish dish quick and easy to prepare.
Serve with your favorite pasta and a green salad.

1 (14- to 16-oz.) jar pasta sauce
6 to 8 fresh mushrooms, sliced
1 tablespoon finely chopped parsley
4 to 6 fish steaks or fillets, about 1 inch thick
2 tablespoons vegetable oil

Combine sauce, mushrooms, and parsley in a medium-size saucepan. Bring to a boil, reduce heat, and simmer 10 to 15 minutes. Preheat broiler. Place fish in oiled broiler pan. Brush top of fish with about half the oil. Broil 4 to 5 inches from heat source about 5 minutes. Turn fish. Brush with remaining oil. Broil 4 minutes or until fish just begins to flake when tested with a fork. Serve sauce over fish. Makes 4 to 6 servings.

Variation

Substitute Double-Tomato Sauce for Fish (page 117) for the pasta sauce.

Pasta & Pizza

Everyone loves pasta and pizza; they are such versatile dishes, combining well with a wide variety of other foods.

Traditionally, spaghetti and lasagne are probably the best-known pasta dishes. Their basic tomato sauces are made in homes and restaurants throughout the country. In addition to these ever-popular favorites, we have included other pasta shapes such as Corkscrews with Tomato Sauce and an Italian-inspired Milanese Special with accents of fennel and pancetta.

Although we suggest a specific kind of pasta with each recipe, you can substitute your favorite shape as long as you use approximately the same size and amount.

Pizza has come a long way since the days of the plain pepperoni and cheese variety. Now, we may start with a base of frozen bread dough or even a shredded zucchini mixture; then build with cheese and other appetizing ingredients. Ready-to-use tomato-based pizza sauces as well as fresh tomatoes make it easy to produce a mouth-watering pizza in minutes.

Corkscrews with Fresh Tomato Sauce

Uncooked fresh plum tomatoes add a refreshing flavor to this easy pasta dish.

8 ounces corkscrew-shaped pasta (about 2 1/2 cups uncooked)
2 tablespoons vegetable oil
1 onion, chopped
1 mild green chile, seeded and chopped
7 or 8 fresh plum tomatoes, diced
1/4 cup chopped cilantro
1/2 teaspoon salt
1 tablespoon white wine Worcestershire sauce
1/4 cup grated Romano cheese or Parmesan cheese
16 thin slices pepperoni (about 1 oz.), coarsely chopped

Cook pasta according to package directions; drain. Rinse with hot water. Drain and set aside. While pasta cooks, heat oil in a large skillet. Add onion and chile. Cook, stirring, 5 minutes or until onion is softened. Remove from heat. Add tomatoes, cilantro, salt, and Worcestershire sauce, then cooked pasta; stir until well blended. Sprinkle with cheese and pepperoni. Toss to combine. Makes 4 or 5 servings.

Creamy Mushroom & Tomato Pasta Shells

For a heartier main dish, stir in three or four slices cooked and crumbled bacon.

8 ounces medium-size pasta shells (about 2 1/2 cups uncooked)
2 tablespoons margarine or butter
8 ounces fresh mushrooms, sliced
1/4 teaspoon salt
1/8 teaspoon freshly ground pepper
2 tablespoons cornstarch
1 cup chicken broth
1 (6-oz.) can tomato paste
1 cup half-and-half
Grated Romano cheese or Parmesan cheese

Cook pasta according to package directions; drain. Rinse with hot water; drain and set aside. While pasta cooks, melt margarine or butter in a large skillet. Add mushrooms, salt, and pepper. Cook, stirring, 2 minutes. Dissolve cornstarch in chicken broth in a small bowl. Stir in tomato paste; add to skillet and cook, stirring, until thickened. Add half-and-half and drained cooked pasta. Sprinkle with cheese. Makes 4 or 5 servings.

Dilled Orzo with Grilled Chicken Salad

You will find orzo in the pasta section of the supermarket. It looks like uncooked rice, but is really a small oval-shaped pasta.

4 boneless chicken breast halves, skinned
1 tablespoon vegetable oil
3/4 cup uncooked orzo
2 medium-size tomatoes, peeled and diced
1 tablespoon chopped chives
3 tablespoons olive oil
1 tablespoon lemon juice
1 tablespoon chopped fresh dill
1/2 teaspoon salt
1/8 teaspoon paprika
1/8 teaspoon freshly ground pepper
Dill sprigs

Preheat grill or broiler. Brush chicken with vegetable oil. Grill or broil about 6 minutes. Turn and brush other side with oil; cook about 5 minutes. Cool; then cube. Cook orzo according to package directions; drain. Combine cooked chicken and cooked orzo in a large bowl. Add tomatoes and chives. Combine olive oil, lemon juice, dill, salt, paprika, and pepper. Pour over chicken and orzo. Toss until well blended. Garnish with dill sprigs. Makes 5 or 6 servings.

Milanese Special

Several classic Italian ingredients are used to create a delicious pasta dish.

1 fennel bulb, very thinly sliced
1 large onion, thinly sliced
4 ounces pancetta, coarsely chopped
1 (28-oz.) can diced peeled tomatoes
1/4 teaspoon salt
1/8 teaspoon freshly ground pepper
8 ounces uncooked linguine or fettuccine
Grated Parmesan cheese or Romano cheese

Combine fennel, onion, pancetta, tomatoes, salt, and pepper in a large skillet. Cover and simmer 30 to 35 minutes or until fennel is softened. Meanwhile cook pasta according to package directions; drain. Rinse and drain again. Add cooked pasta. Sprinkle with cheese; toss to combine. Makes 4 to 6 servings.

Garden-fresh Pasta Platter

*A colorful array of nutritious vegetables, disguised with an appealing
and flavorful sauce over angel hair pasta.*

3 medium-size tomatoes, peeled, seeded, and chopped
1 small onion, finely chopped
2 tablespoons chopped parsley
1 tablespoon Worcestershire sauce
1 garlic clove, crushed
1/2 teaspoon salt
1/8 teaspoon freshly ground pepper
1/2 cup low-fat evaporated milk
2 tablespoons vegetable oil
1 small yellow or red bell pepper, cut into squares
1 small zucchini, diced
8 medium-size mushrooms, quartered
8 ounces fresh angel hair pasta
1/4 cup grated Romano cheese or Parmesan cheese

Simmer tomatoes, onion, parsley, Worcestershire sauce, garlic, salt, and pepper in a 2-quart saucepan 15 minutes. Add milk; heat 2 or 3 minutes. Process in a food processor or blender until pureed. While sauce cooks, heat oil in a 10-inch skillet. Add bell pepper and zucchini. Sauté 5 or 6 minutes. Stir in mushrooms; cook 2 or 3 minutes. Cook pasta according to package directions; drain and arrange on a large platter. Top with vegetables; then tomato sauce. Sprinkle with cheese. Makes 5 or 6 servings.

South of the Border Lasagne

Accompany this hearty dish with a tossed green salad enhanced with chunks of avocado.

8 ounces lasagne noodles
1 pound lean ground beef
2 medium-size tomatoes, chopped
1 onion, chopped
1 green bell pepper, chopped
1 garlic clove, crushed
1 (10- to 12-oz.) jar enchilada sauce
8 ounces ricotta cheese
1 (16-oz.) can chili beans in zesty sauce, undrained
8 ounces jalapeño Jack cheese, shredded (about 2 cups)
Chopped cilantro

Cook lasagne noodles according to package directions; drain. Cover with cold water; drain just before combining with other ingredients. Preheat oven to 350°F (175°C). Lightly brown beef in a large skillet, stirring to break up meat. Add tomatoes, onion, bell pepper, and garlic, cover, and simmer 10 minutes. Stir in enchilada sauce. Arrange one-third of drained noodles on bottom of a 13 × 9-inch baking dish. Spoon one-third of sauce over noodles, then layer one third of the ricotta cheese, beans, and Jack cheese over sauce. Repeat layers, ending with Jack cheese on top. Bake 35 to 40 minutes or until bubbly. Sprinkle with cilantro. Makes 6 to 8 servings.

Fennel, Tomato, & Pasta Toss

Fresh fennel is featured with pasta in a creamy sauce. The feathery tops are used as a garnish. Fennel has a delicate, sweet, mild anise-like flavor.

8 ounces uncooked vermicelli or angel hair pasta
3 tablespoons vegetable oil
1 small fennel bulb, thinly sliced
1 carrot, shredded
1 garlic clove, crushed
3 medium-size tomatoes, peeled, seeded, and coarsely chopped
1/2 teaspoon salt
1/4 teaspoon pepper
1 cup half-and-half or whipping cream
1/2 cup grated Parmesan cheese
1 tablespoon chopped fennel leaves

Cook pasta according to package directions; drain. While pasta cooks, heat oil in a large skillet. Add fennel and carrot; cook over medium heat, stirring occasionally, 15 minutes or until softened. Stir in garlic, tomatoes, salt, and pepper. Cook, stirring, several minutes. Add half-and-half, then cheese. Heat just until hot. Spoon over cooked pasta. Toss until well blended. Sprinkle with chopped fennel leaves. Makes 4 to 6 servings.

Brunch Pasta Pie

The pasta forms the crust for the custardy filling.
Serve for brunch or lunch with crusty bread and a green salad.

4 ounces uncooked vermicelli
2 tablespoons vegetable oil
3 medium-size tomatoes, sliced
3 eggs, slightly beaten
1 cup milk
1 tablespoon Dijon mustard
1/2 teaspoon prepared horseradish
1/4 teaspoon salt
1/8 teaspoon freshly ground black pepper
1/4 cup finely chopped green or yellow bell pepper
1/3 cup thin slivers of pepperoni or salami (1 1/2 to 2 oz.)
1 teaspoon finely chopped parsley

Preheat oven to 350°F (175°C). Cook pasta according to package directions; drain. Add oil; toss pasta until well coated. Press into bottom and sides of a 10-inch shallow baking dish. Top with tomato slices. Combine eggs, milk, mustard, horseradish, salt, and black pepper in a medium-size bowl. Pour over tomatoes in pasta-lined baking dish. Top with bell pepper and pepperoni. Sprinkle with parsley. Bake 35 to 40 minutes or until firm. Makes 6 servings.

Macaroni with Sun-dried Tomatoes & Goat Cheese

Thickened chicken broth forms an appetizing glaze over cooked pasta;
finish with a sprinkling of pine nuts.

8 ounces medium-size elbow macaroni (about 2 1/2 cups uncooked)

2 tablespoons margarine or butter

1 small onion, chopped

1 garlic clove, crushed

1 tablespoon cornstarch

1 cup chicken broth or bouillon

1/4 cup sun-dried tomatoes in oil, drained, chopped

2 tablespoons chopped parsley

2 tablespoons chopped fresh basil

2 ounces goat cheese, coarsely crumbled (about 1/4 cup)

1/4 cup pine nuts, toasted

Cook pasta according to package directions; drain. While pasta cooks, melt margarine in a 10-inch skillet. Add onion and garlic; sauté until softened. Dissolve cornstarch in broth in a small bowl. Add to skillet; stir in sun-dried tomatoes, parsley, and basil. Stir until thickened. Remove from heat. Toss with cooked pasta. Sprinkle top with goat cheese, then pine nuts. Makes 4 or 5 servings.

 Tip

To toast pine nuts, place in a heavy skillet over medium heat. Cook, stirring often, until golden brown.

Easy Pizza-flavored Pasta

All your favorite pizza flavors are tossed with pasta for a quick main dish.

8 ounces wagon-wheel or bow-tie pasta (3 3/4 to 4 cups uncooked)
1 small onion, thinly sliced
1 small green or yellow bell pepper, sliced
1 cup sliced mushrooms (about 4 ounces)
1 garlic clove, crushed
3 ounces pepperoni (about 35 thin slices), halved
1 (6-oz.) can tomato paste
1 1/3 cups beef broth
1 tablespoon chopped fresh basil or 1/2 teaspoon dried leaf basil
1 teaspoon chopped fresh oregano or 1/4 teaspoon dried leaf basil
1/4 teaspoon salt
1/8 teaspoon freshly ground pepper
4 ounces shredded Monterey Jack or mozzarella cheese (1 cup)

Cook pasta according to package directions; drain. Rinse with hot water; drain and set aside. While pasta cooks, combine onion, bell pepper, mushrooms, garlic, pepperoni, tomato paste, broth, basil, oregano, salt, and pepper in a large skillet. Simmer about 5 minutes. Spoon over cooked pasta. Sprinkle with cheese. Toss until well blended. Makes 5 or 6 servings.

Home-style Spaghetti with Meat Sauce

A time-honored favorite with all the aromas of an old-fashioned kitchen,
this contains fresh tomatoes, tomato sauce, and tomato paste.

1 pound lean ground beef
1 medium-size onion, chopped
1 garlic clove, crushed
5 medium-size tomatoes, peeled, seeded, and chopped
1 (8-oz.) can tomato sauce
1 (6-oz.) can tomato paste
2 tablespoons dry red wine
1 tablespoon Worcestershire sauce
2 tablespoons chopped parsley
2 tablespoons chopped fresh basil or 1 teaspoon dried leaf basil
1 teaspoon chopped fresh oregano or 1/4 teaspoon dried leaf oregano
1/2 teaspoon salt
1/8 teaspoon freshly ground pepper
12 ounces spaghetti
Grated Parmesan cheese

Combine beef and onion in a 3- or 4-quart saucepan. Cook over medium heat until browned, stirring occasionally to break up meat. Add garlic, chopped tomatoes, tomato sauce, tomato paste, wine, Worcestershire sauce, parsley, basil, oregano, salt, and pepper. Cover; simmer 30 minutes. While sauce simmers, cook spaghetti according to package directions; drain. Spoon sauce over cooked spaghetti. Sprinkle with cheese. Makes 6 to 8 servings.

 Tip

The sauce can be made ahead and refrigerated up to two days. Bring to a boil before serving.

Turkey Tomato Sauté with Pasta

*Start with ground turkey to create a tempting and low-fat meal-in-a-skillet
that's perfect for a family supper. Serve with steamed broccoli.*

6 ounces pasta corkscrews or twists

1 tablespoon vegetable oil

1 pound ground turkey

1 small onion, chopped

1/2 teaspoon salt

1/8 teaspoon freshly ground black pepper

1 tablespoon minced parsley

2 teaspoons grated ginger root

1 green or yellow bell pepper, sliced

12 to 14 cherry tomatoes, halved

1 cup sliced mushrooms

1/3 cup chicken broth

1/2 cup plain yogurt or sour cream

Cook pasta according to package directions; drain. While pasta cooks, heat oil in a 10-inch skillet. Add turkey, onion, salt, pepper, parsley, and grated ginger. Cook over medium heat until turkey is done, stirring to break up turkey. Add pasta to turkey mixture with bell pepper, tomatoes, mushrooms, broth, and yogurt. Heat until hot and serve. Makes 4 to 6 servings.

Variation

Substitute bulk turkey sausage for the ground turkey. Omit ginger root. Prepare as above.

Bacon, Cheese, & Tomato Pasta Bake

The combination of flavors will remind you of your favorite grilled cheese, bacon, and tomato sandwich. A dry white wine goes well with this dish.

8 ounces medium-size pasta shells
3 bacon slices, chopped
2 tablespoons all-purpose flour
1 cup milk
1/4 teaspoon salt
1/8 teaspoon freshly ground pepper
2 large tomatoes, coarsely chopped
4 ounces shredded Cheddar cheese (1 cup)

Preheat oven to 350°F (175°C). Grease a 2-quart baking dish. Cook pasta according to package directions; drain and set aside. While pasta cooks, cook bacon in a large skillet until crisp; remove with a slotted spoon. Stir flour into skillet. Gradually stir in milk, salt, and pepper; cook, stirring, until thickened. Spoon half the cooked shells into greased baking dish. Add half the bacon and sauce, then half the chopped tomatoes. Repeat layers. Top with cheese. Bake, uncovered, about 20 minutes or until cheese melts and mixture is bubbly. Makes 5 or 6 servings.

Variation

The recipe can be doubled for a large party. Bake in a 13 × 9-inch baking dish.

Pizza Brunch Special

A star performer to impress your family and friends at your next brunch.

1 unbaked refrigerated pie crust
8 ounces pork sausage
5 eggs, slightly beaten
3 tablespoons milk
1/4 teaspoon salt
1/8 teaspoon freshly ground pepper
1/2 cup sliced ripe olives
2 tablespoons sliced green onions
10 to 12 cherry tomatoes, halved
4 ounces shredded mozzarella cheese (1 cup)

Preheat oven to 425°F (220°C). Roll or pat pie crust into a 13-inch round. Press into a 12-inch pizza pan. Fold over edges and flute. Prick bottom with a fork. Bake in preheated oven 12 to 14 minutes or until light brown. While crust bakes, crumble sausage into a hot 8-inch skillet. Cook until done, stirring to break up sausage. Remove sausage with a slotted spoon; drain off all except 1 tablespoon drippings from pan. Set sausage aside. Beat eggs, milk, salt, and pepper in a large bowl. Pour into pan. Cook, stirring, until firm. Spoon scrambled eggs onto baked pastry. Top with cooked sausage, olives, onions, and tomatoes. Sprinkle cheese over all. Return to oven; bake about 5 minutes or until cheese melts. Cut into 6 to 8 wedges.

Variation

The cooked filling can be combined with the toppings and rolled up in warm flour tortillas to make breakfast burritos. Serve with salsa.

Pizza Logs

Reminiscent of calzone, these are good for a family supper or sliced as a party appetizer.
Refrigerated pizza crust makes them quick and easy to make.

4 ounces hot Italian-style turkey sausage
1/2 cup pizza sauce
2 1/2 ounces pepperoni, diced (about 1/2 cup)
1 (4-oz.) can sliced ripe olives, well drained (1/2 cup)
4 ounces shredded mozzarella cheese (1 cup)
1/4 cup grated Parmesan cheese
1 tablespoon cornmeal
1 (10-oz.) can refrigerated pizza crust
1 egg, slightly beaten
1 1/2 teaspoons sesame seeds

Preheat oven to 425°F (220°C). Coat a small skillet with nonstick spray. Remove casing from sausage; crumble into skillet. Cook until lightly browned, stirring to break up meat. Remove from heat; drain off fat, if necessary. Stir in pizza sauce, pepperoni, and olives. Let cool; stir in mozzarella and Parmesan cheeses. Grease a large baking sheet; sprinkle with cornmeal. Unroll dough and with fingers pat out to a thin 15 × 12-inch rectangle. Cut in half lengthwise and into thirds crosswise to make 6 pieces. Spoon 1/2 cup filling along long edge of each rectangle. Gently roll dough over filling to form a 6- or 7-inch log; pinch ends slightly to seal. Place rolls seam side down, 1 inch apart, on prepared baking sheet. Brush with egg, then sprinkle with sesame seeds. Bake 18 to 20 minutes or until golden brown. Cool about 5 minutes on a wire rack; serve warm. Makes 6 logs.

Zucchini Sausage Pizza

A delicious layer of shredded zucchini replaces the traditional pizza crust.
Hot Italian sausage adds a nice spiciness.

1 teaspoon olive oil
8 ounces hot Italian-style sausage links
1 (8-oz.) can tomato sauce
1 teaspoon dried Italian seasoning, crushed
4 cups lightly packed shredded zucchini (about 2 pounds)
1/2 cup finely chopped onion
2 tablespoons minced fresh parsley
8 tablespoons fine dried bread crumbs
8 ounces shredded mozzarella cheese (2 cups)
1 egg, beaten
1/2 teaspoon salt
1/4 teaspoon freshly ground pepper
1/3 cup grated Parmesan cheese

Heat olive oil in a 9-inch skillet over medium-high heat. Remove casings from sausage links; crumble into skillet. Cook until lightly browned, stirring to break up meat. Add tomato sauce and Italian seasoning; remove from heat and set aside. Preheat oven to 350°F (175°C). Combine zucchini, onion, parsley, 6 tablespoons of the bread crumbs, 1 cup of the mozzarella cheese, the egg, salt, and pepper. Mix well. Lightly grease a 12-inch pizza pan; sprinkle with the remaining 2 tablespoons of bread crumbs. Using a spoon, pat zucchini mixture into pizza pan. Sprinkle remaining mozzarella cheese over the zucchini mixture. Spoon tomato-meat mixture evenly over mozzarella cheese, covering as much as possible. Sprinkle with Parmesan cheese. Bake 30 to 35 minutes or until golden. Let stand 5 to 10 minutes. Cut into wedges. Makes 6 servings.

Deep-Dish Pizza

The crust of this version is slightly thicker than the traditional pizza; it has a biscuitlike texture.

1 cup all-purpose flour
1 1/2 teaspoons baking powder
1/2 teaspoon salt
1/4 cup margarine or butter, chilled
1 large egg, beaten
1/2 cup milk
1 1/2 tablespoons cornmeal
6 ounces shredded mozzarella cheese (1 1/2 cups)
1 1/2 ounces thinly sliced pepperoni (16 to 18 slices)
1 cup sliced fresh mushrooms
1/2 cup diced green bell pepper
1 (14-oz.) jar pizza sauce (1 1/2 to 1 2/3 cups)
1/4 cup grated Parmesan cheese

Preheat oven to 425°F (220°C). Combine flour, baking powder, and salt in a medium-size bowl. Cut in margarine until mixture resembles cornmeal. Stir in egg and milk to form a thick batter. Lightly oil a 9-inch round baking pan. Sprinkle with cornmeal, coating bottom and side. Spread batter evenly over bottom of pan. Sprinkle mozzarella cheese over batter. Top with pepperoni, mushrooms, and bell pepper. Spoon pizza sauce over all. Sprinkle with Parmesan cheese. Bake 20 to 25 minutes or until browned and bubbly. Let stand 5 to 10 minutes; cut into wedges. Makes 6 servings.

Variation

Substitute the meat sauce (page 64) for the pizza sauce.

Chili Pizza

*Frozen bread dough thaws in one to two hours at room temperature
or six to eight hours in the refrigerator.*

1 (1-lb.) loaf frozen bread dough
2 tablespoons vegetable oil
1 (15-oz.) can chili without beans
3 small plum tomatoes, thinly sliced
1 small green bell pepper, diced
3 small green onions, including tops, thinly sliced
4 ounces shredded Cheddar cheese (about 1 cup)
4 ounces shredded mozzarella cheese (about 1 cup)
1 teaspoon dried leaf oregano, crushed

Brush frozen bread dough with oil; thaw. Preheat oven to 425°F (220°C). Lightly grease a 12-inch pizza pan. With fingers, pat thawed dough out to a 12-inch round on pizza pan. Spread chili over dough to within 1/2 inch of edge. Top with tomato slices, bell pepper, and green onions. Combine the cheeses and sprinkle evenly over top. Sprinkle with oregano. Bake 20 minutes or until browned and bubbly. Cut into 8 wedges.

Breads & Sandwiches

Many people are fascinated with breads—whether they are homemade or dressed-up bakery selections. We have included a wide variety, ranging from muffins to filled pita bread.

Homemade Tomato Cheese Muffins and Tomato-Speckled Rosemary Scones win blue ribbons for homemade quick breads. Just add a little margarine or butter, and you're all set for a delicious treat.

For sandwiches, we have chosen some of your favorite fillings at the deli or supermarket; other sandwiches are stuffed with creative combinations that taste exotic but can be put together in minutes. Cut-up fresh tomatoes are starred in the popular Italian-style bruschetta made with French bread and seasoned with fresh basil, parsley, chives, and garlic.

Pesto Pine-Nut Loaf

*This delicious quick bread may be served warm or cool; it is even better
when spread with softened cream cheese or butter.*

2 cups all-purpose flour
2 teaspoons baking powder
1/2 teaspoon baking soda
4 ounces shredded Monterey Jack cheese (1 cup)
1 tablespoon finely chopped fresh basil
1/4 teaspoon seasoned salt
1 tablespoon finely chopped parsley
1/4 cup sun-dried tomatoes in oil, drained and chopped
1 tablespoon finely chopped green onion
2 eggs, slightly beaten
2 tablespoons vegetable oil
1 cup milk
2 tablespoons pine nuts

Preheat oven to 350°F (175°C). Grease a 9-inch loaf pan. Combine flour, baking powder, soda, cheese, basil, seasoned salt, parsley, sun-dried tomatoes, and green onion in a large bowl. In another bowl, combine eggs, oil, and milk. Stir egg mixture into flour mixture just until combined. Pour into prepared pan; sprinkle top with pine nuts. Bake about 40 minutes or until a wooden pick inserted in the center comes out clean. Cool in pan 5 minutes. Invert on a rack to cool completely. Cut into slices to serve. Makes 1 loaf.

Chang Mai Pita Pockets

An enticing combination of ingredients with a Southeast Asia flavor makes this one of my favorites.

1 pound boneless pork loin
2 tablespoons vegetable oil
1 tablespoon cornstarch
1/3 cup chicken bouillon or broth
1 tablespoon finely chopped crystallized ginger
1 tablespoon soy sauce
1 tablespoon Dijon mustard
1 cup snow peas, halved crosswise
1/2 cup sliced water chestnuts
14 to 15 cherry tomatoes, halved or quartered
4 pita breads, halved crosswise
Toasted sesame seeds

Cut pork into thin strips. Heat oil in a 10-inch skillet. Add pork; cook and stir about 5 minutes. Combine cornstarch, chicken bouillon, ginger, soy sauce, and mustard in a small bowl. Add to pan. Cook, stirring, until thickened. Stir in snow peas, water chestnuts, and cherry tomatoes. Spoon about 1/2 cup of this mixture into each pita bread half. Sprinkle with sesame seeds. Makes 8 filled pita pocket halves.

Grilled Deli Pocket Sandwiches

For a complete meal, serve this hearty sandwich with cole slaw or a vegetable salad.

4 pita bread rounds
1 small garlic clove, crushed
2 tablespoons margarine or butter, melted
8 ounces very thinly sliced roast beef or ham
3 medium-size tomatoes, thinly sliced
Salt and freshly ground pepper (optional)
8 ounces shredded sharp Cheddar cheese (2 cups)

With a sharp knife, split each pita into 2 rounds. Combine garlic with margarine in a small bowl. Brush the smooth outer side of each round with margarine mixture. For each sandwich, top two of the rounds, inside up, equally with slices of roast beef and tomatoes. Sprinkle lightly with salt and pepper, if desired. Sprinkle equal amounts of cheese over each sandwich, then top with matching pita round, smooth side up. Grill sandwiches in a skillet or griddle over medium-high heat until golden brown, about 2 minutes on each side. With a sharp knife, cut sandwiches in half and serve immediately. Makes 4 servings.

Spinach & Egg Brunch Muffins

These are perfect knife-and-fork open-face sandwiches for a weekend brunch, or a special weekday breakfast when you're tired of your traditional fare.

1 (9 1/2- to 10-oz.) package frozen creamed spinach
3 hard-cooked eggs, peeled and chopped
4 bacon slices, crisp-cooked
1 green onion, finely chopped
1 teaspoon Worcestershire sauce
6 English muffin halves, toasted
2 medium-size tomatoes, chopped
3 ounces shredded mozzarella cheese (3/4 cup)

Preheat broiler. Cook spinach according to package directions. Combine cooked spinach, eggs, bacon, onion, and Worcestershire sauce in a small bowl. Spoon about 1/4 cup spinach mixture on each toasted muffin half. Top each with equal amounts of chopped tomatoes, then cheese. Place muffin halves on a baking sheet. Broil until cheese melts. Makes 6 servings.

Variation

If creamed spinach is not available, cook one (10-oz.) package frozen chopped spinach according to package directions. Drain well and stir spinach, eggs, bacon, onion, and Worcestershire sauce into 2 cups medium white sauce made using 4 tablespoons flour, 4 tablespoons butter, and 2 cups milk.

Chile Corn Bread

This fairly dense bread is practically a complete meal; serve it with a large green salad.

1 cup yellow cornmeal
1 cup all-purpose flour
2 teaspoons baking powder
1 teaspoon baking soda
1/2 teaspoon salt
2 eggs, slightly beaten
1/2 cup dairy sour cream
1 (8-oz.) can cream-style corn
1/4 cup chopped sun-dried tomatoes
1/4 cup vegetable oil
1 (4-oz.) can chopped green chiles or jalapeño chiles, drained
2 ounces shredded Cheddar cheese (1/2 cup)

Preheat oven to 400°F (205°C). Grease a round 9-inch cake pan or baking dish. Combine cornmeal, flour, baking powder, soda, and salt in a medium-size bowl. In another bowl, combine eggs, sour cream, corn, sun-dried tomatoes, vegetable oil, and chiles. Pour into dry ingredients; stir just until moistened. Spoon batter into prepared pan. Bake 25 to 35 minutes or until a wooden pick inserted in center comes out clean. Immediately, sprinkle with cheese. Let stand 2 or 3 minutes; cut into wedges. Makes 6 to 8 servings.

Taste of Tuscany Bruschetta

This popular and colorful Italian herbed bread can be served as an appetizer or as a sandwich.

6 medium-size tomatoes, finely chopped
1/4 cup finely chopped fresh basil leaves
1 tablespoon chopped chives
1 tablespoon finely chopped parsley
1/4 teaspoon salt
1/8 teaspoon freshly ground pepper
2 garlic cloves, halved
1/2 cup extra-virgin olive oil
1 (1-lb.) loaf French bread, cut crosswise into 16 slices

Combine tomatoes, basil, chives, parsley, salt, and pepper in a medium-size bowl. Cover and let stand at room temperature at least 1 hour. Combine garlic and olive oil in a small bowl. Cover and let stand at room temperature at least 1 hour. Toast bread on both sides. Brush with garlic-flavored oil. Spoon tomato mixture on top of bread slices. Arrange on a serving tray and serve immediately. Makes 16 slices.

Tomato-speckled Rosemary Scones

The flavors of sun-dried tomatoes, garlic, and fresh rosemary make this an unusually delicious quick bread. Serve with a main-dish salad or as part of a tea.

2 cups all-purpose flour
1 tablespoon baking powder
1/2 teaspoon salt
1/3 cup diced sun-dried tomatoes
2 garlic cloves, minced
2 teaspoons minced fresh rosemary
1/3 cup olive oil
1 cup milk

Preheat oven to 450°F (230°C). Combine flour, baking powder, and salt in a medium-size bowl. Stir in tomatoes, garlic, and rosemary. Combine oil and milk in another bowl. Pour milk mixture all at once into flour mixture. Stir until well mixed to make a soft dough. Drop by 6 large spoonfuls (about 1/3 cup each) onto an ungreased baking sheet. Bake 12 to 15 minutes or until golden brown. Serve hot. Makes 6 large scones.

Tomato Cheese Muffins

Old-fashioned muffins with a new flavor, these are a wonderful accompaniment to grilled pork or beef.

2 1/2 cups all-purpose flour
1 1/2 teaspoons baking powder
1/2 teaspoon baking soda
1 teaspoon instant minced onion
1/2 teaspoon salt
2 tablespoons sugar
1 tablespoon chopped fresh basil or 1 teaspoon dried leaf basil
2 eggs, slightly beaten
1 medium-size tomato, peeled, seeded, and chopped
1/2 cup milk
2 tablespoons ketchup
1/4 cup margarine or butter, melted
3 ounces shredded Cheddar cheese (3/4 cup)

Preheat oven to 375°F (190°C). Line 12 muffin cups with fluted paper liners or grease 12 muffin cups; set aside. Combine flour, baking powder, soda, instant onion, salt, sugar, and basil in a medium-size bowl. Combine eggs, tomato, milk, ketchup, and margarine in another bowl. Add tomato mixture and 1/2 cup of the cheese to dry ingredients; stir until just moistened. Spoon equal amounts into prepared muffin cups. Sprinkle tops with remaining 1/4 cup cheese. Bake about 18 minutes or until golden brown. Serve warm. Makes 12 muffins.

Variation

These can also be baked in mini-muffin cups. Reduce baking time to about 10 minutes.

Baked Tomato & Cheese Sandwiches

Great for brunch, lunch, or a midnight snack, this warm sandwich is somewhat reminiscent of Welsh rarebit but with tomatoes and bacon.

3 tablespoons margarine or butter
3 tablespoons all-purpose flour
1/2 teaspoon dry mustard
1/4 teaspoon salt
1/8 teaspoon ground white pepper
1 cup milk
4 rye bread or French bread slices, 1/2 inch thick, toasted
8 tomato slices, 1/4 inch thick
4 bacon slices, crisp-cooked and crumbled
4 ounces shredded Swiss cheese (1 cup)
Paprika

Preheat oven to 350°F (175°C). Melt margarine in a medium-size saucepan over low heat; blend in flour, dry mustard, salt, and pepper. Cook, stirring, until smooth and bubbly. Stir in milk. Cook over medium heat, stirring constantly, until thickened. Set aside. Place toast on a baking sheet. Top each slice of toast with 2 tomato slices, then one-fourth of the crumbled bacon and 1/4 cup sauce. Top each with 1/4 cup of the cheese and a dash of paprika. Bake 20 minutes or until heated. Makes 4 sandwiches.

Variation

Substitute shredded Cheddar cheese for the Swiss cheese.

Cracker Bread Roll-up

*It's important to soften the crisp cracker bread until it is soft and pliable
so that it can be rolled without cracking.*

1 large cracker bread or lahvosh (about a 14-inch round)
1 (8-oz.) package cream cheese, softened
4 ounces feta cheese, crumbled
2 teaspoons grated lemon peel
1 tablespoon lemon juice
1 teaspoon dried leaf oregano, crushed
1 teaspoon dried dill weed
1/2 teaspoon freshly ground black pepper
8 ounces very thinly sliced deli roast beef
2 medium-size firm ripe tomatoes, thinly sliced
2 cups lightly packed shredded romaine lettuce
1 small cucumber, cut into very thin slices
1 (4-oz.) can sliced ripe olives, well drained (1/2 cup)
1/2 cup diced green bell pepper (optional)

Thoroughly wet both sides of cracker bread or lahvosh by holding under cold running water. Place between 2 damp towels for 45 to 60 minutes to soften. Dampen again, if necessary. Mix together cream cheese, feta cheese, lemon peel, lemon juice, oregano, dill, and black pepper in a medium-size bowl. Place softened bread on an 18-inch piece of plastic wrap or foil. Spread bread with cheese mixture. Top with roast beef, tomatoes, lettuce, cucumber, olives, and bell pepper, if using. Roll up tightly jellyroll fashion. Wrap in plastic wrap or foil; refrigerate up to 8 hours. Cut with a sharp knife into 12 thick slices. Makes 12 rolled sandwiches or 6 servings.

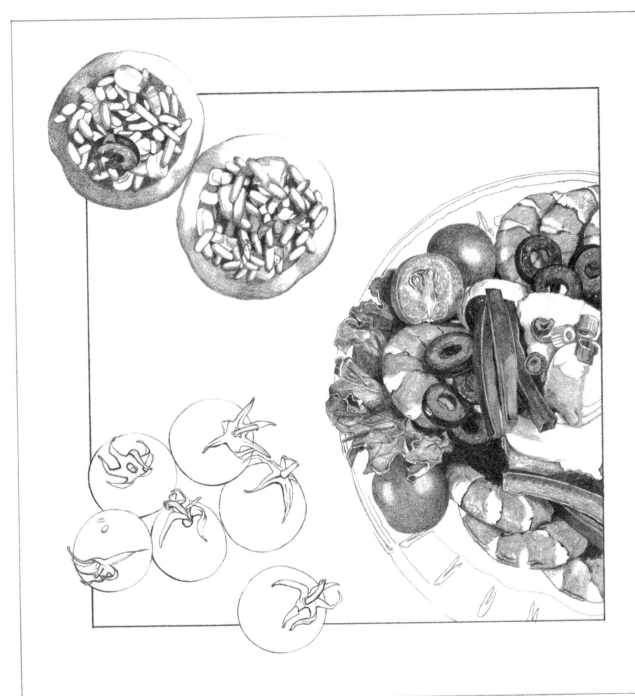

Salads & Salad Dressings

This tempting collection of salads includes many perennial favorites that feature tomatoes. That's because tomatoes are so versatile and blend well with such a wide variety of foods. Tomatoes assume many shapes when used in salads. They may be scooped out, then used as cups filled with various combinations of vegetables, chicken, or cheese with mayonnaise or sour cream. Or wedges of tomatoes provide a colorful and delicious accent in a tossed green salad. Chopped pieces of tomatoes complement the corn and black beans in our Corn, Bean, & Tomato Bowl. For a slightly different accent of color and flavor, try the Venetian Shrimp Bowl with thin wedges of plum tomatoes.

Corn, Bean, & Tomato Bowl

Take it to your next picnic or potluck; top with corn chips at the last minute.

1 (10- to 12-oz.) can whole-kernel corn, drained
1 (15- to 16-oz.) can black beans, drained
1 small cucumber, peeled and diced
3 medium-size tomatoes, coarsely chopped
2 green onions, chopped
1/4 cup vegetable oil
2 tablespoons red wine vinegar
1 teaspoon Worcestershire sauce
2 tablespoons ketchup
1 tablespoon honey
1 tablespoon prepared mustard
1 teaspoon soy sauce
1/2 cup coarsely crumbled corn chips

Combine corn, beans, cucumber, tomatoes, and green onions in a large bowl. Whisk together oil, vinegar, Worcestershire sauce, ketchup, honey, mustard, and soy sauce in a small bowl. Pour dressing over vegetable mixture; toss to combine. Sprinkle with crumbled corn chips. Makes about 4 to 6 servings.

Amalfi Salad

A very simple, yet impressive salad for a first course or a main dish for a special luncheon.

3 large tomatoes
1 (14-oz.) jar or can artichoke hearts in water, drained and halved
1 small red onion, thinly sliced
6 anchovies, finely chopped
3 tablespoons olive oil
2 tablespoons balsamic vinegar
1 garlic clove, crushed
1 tablespoon chopped fresh parsley
1/8 teaspoon freshly ground pepper
6 to 8 Boston or Bibb lettuce leaves

Cut each tomato into 8 wedges. Combine in a large bowl with artichoke hearts and red onion. Whisk together anchovies, oil, vinegar, garlic, parsley, and pepper in a small bowl. Pour over tomato mixture; toss until combined. Line a shallow salad bowl or individual salad plates with Boston or Bibb lettuce. Spoon tomato mixture over lettuce. Makes 6 servings.

Variation

Substitute 1 carton small red pear tomatoes for the large tomatoes. Cut any large tomatoes in half.

Multilayered Salad Toss

This salad is so attractive that you will want to use your prettiest glass bowl to show it off.

2 medium-size tomatoes, peeled and cubed
1 cup small cubes Monterey Jack cheese
4 slices cooked ham, julienned (about 3 oz.)
1 (15- or 16-oz.) can small red beans, drained
2 green onions, sliced
1 small yellow or red bell pepper, julienned
3 cups shredded lettuce or mixed greens
1/3 cup olive oil
1/4 cup white wine vinegar
1 garlic clove, crushed
1 tablespoon finely chopped cilantro leaves
1/2 teaspoon salt
1/8 teaspoon freshly ground black pepper
1 avocado or sliced ripe olives

Make layers of tomatoes, cheese, ham, beans, green onions, bell pepper, and lettuce in a 2 1/2-quart glass salad bowl, starting with tomatoes and ending with lettuce. Serve at once or cover and refrigerate up to 3 hours. Whisk together oil, vinegar, garlic, cilantro, salt, and black pepper in a small bowl. Pour dressing over layered salad; toss to combine. Peel, pit, and slice avocado. Garnish salad with avocado slices. Makes about 6 servings.

Tortellini Vegetable Combo

*Gently pull a vegetable peeler across the surface of a chunk of
Parmesan cheese to make slightly curled shavings.*

1 (8- to 9-oz.) package fresh or frozen chicken and prosciutto tortellini
1 (16-oz.) package frozen mixed vegetables
1 cup cherry tomatoes, halved (about 12 tomatoes)
1/3 cup vegetable oil
2 tablespoons white wine vinegar
1 teaspoon lemon juice
1 tablespoon Dijon mustard
1/4 teaspoon salt
1/8 teaspoon freshly ground pepper
1/4 cup thinly shaved Parmesan cheese

Cook tortellini and frozen vegetables according to package directions; drain. Cool tortellini and vegetables; combine with tomatoes in a large bowl. Whisk together oil, vinegar, lemon juice, mustard, salt, and pepper in a small bowl. Pour dressing over vegetable mixture; toss to combine. Top salad with shaved cheese. Makes 4 to 5 servings.

Wild West Toss

An attractive, colorful salad that can be made ahead, then transported to a picnic or barbecue.

3 medium-size tomatoes, chopped
1 small red onion, chopped
1 small yellow or green bell pepper, chopped
1 (28-oz.) can pinto beans, drained
1 cup diced cooked ham (about 5 oz.)
1 tablespoon chopped fresh basil
2 tablespoons vegetable oil
2 tablespoons red wine vinegar
1/2 teaspoon chili powder
1/4 teaspoon salt
1/8 teaspoon freshly ground black pepper
2 tablespoons grated Parmesan cheese

Combine tomatoes, onion, bell pepper, beans, ham, and basil in a large bowl. Whisk together oil, vinegar, chili powder, salt, and black pepper in a small bowl. Pour dressing over bean mixture; toss to combine. Sprinkle cheese over salad. Makes about 4 main-dish servings or about 8 side-salad servings.

Venetian Shrimp Bowl

This delicious combination of shrimp and cannellini beans makes a salad
that's hearty enough to be featured as a main dish.

12 ounces cooked shelled medium-size shrimp, halved lengthwise
1 (16-oz.) can cannellini beans, drained
4 large plum tomatoes, cut into thin wedges
2 green onions, sliced
1 tablespoon chopped fresh basil
1/4 cup olive oil
2 tablespoons lemon juice
1 tablespoon Dijon mustard
1 garlic clove, crushed
1/4 teaspoon salt
1/8 teaspoon freshly ground pepper
Ripe olives

Combine shrimp, beans, tomatoes, onions, and basil in a large bowl. Whisk together oil, lemon juice, mustard, garlic, salt, and pepper in a small bowl. Pour dressing over shrimp mixture; toss until well coated. Garnish with ripe olives. Makes 4 to 6 servings.

Gazpacho Salad

Make an exciting salad with the same flavors that you enjoy in the ever-popular cold soup.

2 medium-size tomatoes, chopped
1 cucumber, peeled, seeded, and chopped
1 yellow bell pepper, chopped
1/2 cup chopped Vidalia, Maui, or other mild onion
3 tablespoons vegetable oil
2 tablespoons red wine vinegar
1 garlic clove, crushed
1/4 teaspoon salt
1 teaspoon Worcestershire sauce
2 or 3 dashes of hot pepper sauce
3/4 cup herb-flavored croutons

Combine tomatoes, cucumber, bell pepper, and onion in a medium-size bowl. Whisk together oil, vinegar, garlic, salt, Worcestershire sauce, and hot sauce in a small bowl. Pour dressing over vegetables. Serve at once or cover and refrigerate up to 2 hours. Top with croutons just before serving. Makes 4 or 5 servings.

Pesto Pasta in Tomato Shells

Impressive and refreshing yet filling individual salads for a hot summer day.

1 cup small pasta shells (4 oz. uncooked)
6 large tomatoes
1/3 cup loosely packed fresh basil leaves
1/4 cup grated Parmesan cheese or Romano cheese
1 garlic clove
3 tablespoons olive oil
1/4 teaspoon salt
1/8 teaspoon freshly ground pepper
2 tablespoons pine nuts
Lettuce leaves

Cook pasta according to package directions; drain and rinse with cold water. Set aside. Cut off a slice about 1/2 inch thick across top of each tomato. With a spoon, scoop out seeds, pulp, and juice, leaving tomato shells. Use inside pulp for another purpose. Turn tomato shells upside down on paper towels. Combine basil, cheese, garlic, olive oil, salt, and pepper in a blender or food processor; process until almost smooth. Combine with cooked pasta and pine nuts. Spoon into drained tomato shells. Arrange lettuce on 6 salad plates. Place a filled tomato on each plate. Makes 6 servings.

Unbelievable Molded Salad

*When you serve this salad, the unusual flavor combinations will
keep everyone guessing about the ingredients.*

1 (6-oz.) package raspberry-flavored gelatin
1 (14- to 15-oz.) can stewed tomatoes
1 (12-oz.) jar picante sauce
Lettuce or mixed greens

Horseradish Dressing:

1 cup plain low-fat yogurt
1 tablespoon prepared horseradish

Pour gelatin into a heatproof bowl. Bring stewed tomatoes to a boil in a small saucepan. Pour hot tomatoes over gelatin; stir until dissolved. Stir in picante sauce. Pour into 1-quart mold. Cover and refrigerate until firm, about 4 hours. Unmold salad on serving plate (see Tip). Garnish salad with lettuce. Serve with dressing. Makes 6 to 8 servings.

Horseradish Dressing

Combine yogurt and horseradish in a small bowl. Serve with salad.

Tip

To unmold a gelatin salad, first loosen salad from edge of mold with the tip of a knife. Shake mold gently. Dip mold to depth of contents in warm not hot water 4 or 5 seconds. Invert a dampened serving plate over top of mold. Holding firmly together, flip so salad is right side up. Shake gently to release salad from mold.

Roasted Eggplant & Goat Cheese Salad

Japanese eggplant is smaller and thinner than the traditional eggplant, and just right for these salads.

2 Japanese or oriental eggplants (5 to 6 oz. each)
2 tablespoons olive oil
1/4 teaspoon salt
1/8 teaspoon freshly ground pepper
1 (7-oz.) package goat cheese
2 tablespoons chopped mixed fresh herbs
6 cups mixed greens
3/4 cup Tomato Vinaigrette (page 96)

Preheat oven to 375°F (190°C). Trim ends off eggplants; cut each lengthwise into 6 long slices. Lightly brush both sides with olive oil. Arrange slices in a single layer on a baking sheet. Sprinkle with salt and pepper. Bake eggplant slices until tender, about 15 minutes. Let stand until cool enough to handle. Divide goat cheese into 12 portions. Place 1 portion at end of each eggplant slice. Top each with 1/2 teaspoon herbs. Roll up and place seam side down. Arrange 1 cup of greens on each salad plate. Top with 2 eggplant rolls; drizzle 2 tablespoons Tomato Vinaigrette over each serving. Makes 6 servings.

Green Tomato Dressing

Keep your family and friends guessing about the ingredients in this deliciously unusual dressing.

1 large green tomato, cored and quartered
3/4 cup light mayonnaise
2 green onions, coarsely chopped
1 garlic clove, quartered
1/4 cup loosely packed parsley
2 tablespoons coarsely chopped fresh tarragon
1 tablespoon white wine vinegar
1/4 teaspoon salt
1/8 teaspoon freshly ground pepper

Place all ingredients in a blender or food processor; process until ingredients are finely chopped but not pureed. Serve as a salad dressing for greens or as a dip for corn chips. Makes 2 cups.

Tomato Vinaigrette

The addition of sun-dried tomatoes intensifies the tomato flavor of this rosy salad dressing.

2/3 cup tomato juice
1/3 cup extra-virgin olive oil
1/4 cup red wine vinegar
2 small garlic cloves, crushed
1 teaspoon dried leaf basil, crushed
1/2 teaspoon dried leaf oregano, crushed
1/4 teaspoon dried leaf marjoram, crushed

1/2 teaspoon salt
1/2 teaspoon freshly ground black pepper
2 tablespoons minced sun-dried tomatoes

Whisk all ingredients together in a small bowl until well blended. Cover and refrigerate at least 1 hour before using. Dressing can be refrigerated in a covered glass container up to 1 week. Makes 1 1/3 cups dressing.

Tomato Herb Dressing

Dressing will thicken as it stands; stir just before using.

2 small tomatoes, peeled and seeded
1 teaspoon chopped chives
2 teaspoons chopped parsley
1/4 teaspoon dried leaf marjoram
1/2 teaspoon sugar
1/4 teaspoon salt
1/8 teaspoon freshly ground pepper
1 tablespoon red wine vinegar
1/4 cup olive oil or vegetable oil

Combine all ingredients except oil in a blender or food processor. Process until tomatoes are finely chopped but not pureed. Stir in oil. Serve or cover and refrigerate up to 3 days. Use as a dressing for green or mixed vegetable salads. Makes 1 cup.

Vegetable Treats

Colorful bright red tomatoes are showoffs. This is especially true when they are paired with compatible vegetables such as corn or eggplant. The result is a vegetable with lots of appetite appeal in addition to eye appeal.

Gorgonzola Grilled Tomatoes are one of our favorite vegetable dishes. They go quite well with grilled meats. Best of all, they are quick and easy to do, yet have an interesting character of their own. Last but not least are two recipes for fried green tomatoes. One is fried with a batter coating, the other with a crumb texture. Try both to see which is your favorite.

Scalloped Fresh Tomatoes

A popular flavor combination with time-saving herb-flavored ingredients.

6 medium-size tomatoes, peeled, seeded, and cubed
3 cups seasoned or herb-flavored croutons
2 tablespoons finely chopped green onion
2 tablespoons finely chopped parsley
1/4 teaspoon seasoned salt
2 tablespoons margarine or butter, melted
2 tablespoons grated Parmesan cheese or Romano cheese

Preheat oven to 350°F (175°C). Spoon half the tomatoes into a 1 3/4- or 2-quart baking dish. Top with half the croutons, then remaining tomatoes. Sprinkle with green onion, parsley, and seasoned salt, then with remaining croutons. Drizzle margarine over top. Sprinkle with cheese. Bake, uncovered, 25 to 30 minutes or until bubbly around edges. Makes 6 to 8 servings.

Picante Eggplant & Tomatoes

Ready-to-serve picante sauce is available at your supermarket in a variety of sizes of glass jars. Serve with grilled fish or chicken.

1 medium-size eggplant, cut into strips about 1 × 1/4 inch
1 teaspoon salt
2 tablespoons olive or vegetable oil
1 small onion, chopped
2 medium-size tomatoes, diced

1 tablespoon finely chopped fresh basil
1/4 teaspoon finely chopped fresh rosemary
1 cup picante sauce
4 ounces shredded mozzarella cheese (1 cup)

Place eggplant in a colander; sprinkle with salt. Let drain about 30 minutes. Heat oil in a 10-inch skillet. Add eggplant. Cook, stirring occasionally, about 10 minutes or until eggplant is softened. Add onion, tomatoes, basil, rosemary, and picante sauce. Simmer, stirring, 2 or 3 minutes. Sprinkle with mozzarella cheese. Makes 4 to 6 servings.

Herbed Broiled Tomatoes

Tomato halves should be level to hold herb mixture; if they're not, cut a thin slice off the bottom of each. Make these when you are using the broiler to broil meat or fish.

3 medium-size tomatoes, halved crosswise
2/3 cup fresh bread crumbs
1 teaspoon finely chopped parsley
2 tablespoons butter or margarine, softened
1/4 teaspoon dried leaf marjoram
1/4 teaspoon seasoned salt

Preheat broiler. Place tomatoes cut side up on broiler pan. Combine bread crumbs, parsley, butter, marjoram, and seasoned salt in a small bowl. Spoon equal amounts of topping on the cut side of each tomato. Broil about 4 inches from source of heat about 2 minutes or until topping is lightly browned. Makes 6 servings.

Gorgonzola Grilled Tomatoes

Especially good with barbecued or grilled meats and poultry, these are best when made with garden-ripened tomatoes.

3 large tomatoes
2 tablespoons olive oil
1/2 cup crumbled Gorgonzola cheese (about 3 oz.)
2 teaspoons chopped chives
1 tablespoon milk
1/4 cup fresh bread crumbs

Halve tomatoes crosswise; score cut sides. Brush cut side of each with olive oil. Heat a grill or skillet. Combine cheese, chives, milk, and bread crumbs in a small bowl. Place tomatoes cut side down on hot grill or skillet. Cook about 2 minutes. Turn tomatoes cut side up. Spoon cheese mixture equally on top of each. Cook 1 or 2 minutes. Serve warm. Makes 6 servings.

Tomato Curry with Brown Rice

A special treat for those who enjoy spicy food. Serve as a side dish with a pork roast.

1/4 cup margarine or butter
2 large onions, chopped
3 large garlic cloves, minced
2 tablespoons curry powder
1 teaspoon salt
1/2 teaspoon red (cayenne) pepper or to taste
1/4 teaspoon ground turmeric
12 medium-size tomatoes, peeled, seeded, and cut into 8 wedges each
1/4 cup water

5 to 6 cups cooked brown rice
Small bowls of shredded coconut, chutney, chopped peanuts, and sliced green onions

Melt margarine in a large heavy skillet. Add chopped onions, garlic, curry powder, salt, cayenne, and turmeric; cook about 3 minutes or until onions are softened. Stir in tomatoes and water. Cook over low heat, uncovered, 15 to 20 minutes or until tomatoes are tender, stirring occasionally. Serve hot over cooked brown rice. Pass bowls of coconut, chutney, peanuts, and green onions. Makes 5 or 6 servings.

Corn Custard Tomato Cups

This updated version of corn pudding is baked in a tomato shell.
Do not overcook these or the tomatoes will fall apart.

4 tomatoes (6 to 7 oz. each)
2 eggs
1 teaspoon sugar
1/4 teaspoon salt
1/8 teaspoon freshly ground pepper
1 (8-oz.) can whole-kernel corn, well drained
1 teaspoon minced onion
1/3 cup fresh milk or evaporated milk
1 ounce shredded Swiss cheese (1/4 cup)
Chopped parsley

Cut off a slice about 1/2 inch thick across the top of each tomato. With a spoon, scoop out and discard all seeds and pulp, leaving tomato shell. Turn upside down to drain on paper towels. Preheat oven to 325°F (165°C). Beat eggs in a medium-size bowl until lemon-colored. Beat in sugar, salt, and pepper. Stir in corn, onion, and milk. Place each well-drained tomato cut side up in a 6-ounce glass baking cup. Fill each tomato shell with corn mixture. Bake 45 to 55 minutes or just until a knife inserted off-center in filling comes out clean. Top each tomato with cheese and chopped parsley. Makes 4 servings.

Tomato Risotto

It is important to use arborio rice for a creamy Italian-type risotto.

1 (14 1/2-oz.) can diced tomatoes in tomato juice
2 cups chicken broth
2 tablespoons vegetable oil
1 medium-size onion, diced
1 cup arborio rice
1/4 cup grated Parmesan cheese
2 teaspoons finely chopped fresh basil

Combine tomatoes and juice with broth in a 1 1/2-quart pan and bring to a boil. Cover and keep hot. Heat oil in a 10-inch skillet. Add onion; sauté 2 or 3 minutes or until softened. Add rice and sauté 2 or 3 minutes. Pour in 1/2 cup of the very hot tomato-broth mixture. Stir constantly over medium heat until liquid is absorbed but mixture is not dry. Continue adding 1/2 cup hot liquid at a time; cooking and stirring until all is added and rice is creamy and tender. Stir in Parmesan cheese; top with fresh basil. Makes about 4 servings.

Spanish Rice Skillet with Vegetables

Vegetable lovers' special—Spanish rice flavors are combined with garden vegetables.
Serve with your favorite Mexican dishes or roasted chicken.

2 bacon slices, chopped
1 onion, chopped
1/2 cup chopped celery
3/4 cup long-grain white rice
1 cup water
1 (14 1/2-oz.) can beef broth
1 (16-oz.) can tomato puree
1 tablespoon Worcestershire sauce
1/2 teaspoon chili powder
1/2 teaspoon salt
1/8 teaspoon freshly ground pepper
1 (10-oz.) package frozen green peas
1 cup sliced mushrooms

Cook bacon in a 10-inch skillet until almost crisp. Stir in onion and celery; cook another 2 or 3 minutes. Add rice, water, broth, puree, Worcestershire sauce, chili powder, salt, and pepper. Bring to a boil. Reduce heat, cover, and simmer about 30 minutes or until rice is almost tender. Stir in peas and mushrooms; cover and cook another 10 to 15 minutes or until rice is tender and liquid is absorbed. Makes about 6 servings.

Batter-fried Green Tomatoes

If you have an electric deep-fryer, follow manufacturer's directions for its use. The oil temperature in this recipe is lower than usual for deep-frying because of the high moisture content of the tomatoes.

1 cup all-purpose flour
2/3 cup cornmeal
2 tablespoons sugar
1 1/2 teaspoons baking powder
1/2 teaspoon salt
2 tablespoons vegetable oil
1 cup milk
1 egg, slightly beaten
2 cups vegetable oil for deep-frying
3 medium-size green tomatoes, cut into 1/2-inch slices

Combine flour, cornmeal, sugar, baking powder, and salt in a medium-size bowl. Combine the 2 tablespoons oil, milk, and egg in a small bowl. Stir egg mixture into flour mixture. Heat the 2 cups oil to 325°F (165°C) in a heavy 2-quart pan. Dip tomato slices into batter, shaking off excess batter. Carefully place battered slices into hot oil. Fry until golden or about 1 minute on each side. Drain on paper towels. Makes about 15 slices.

Dixie Fried Green Tomatoes

A traditional Southern favorite that's popular everywhere. It is the cornmeal that adds the Southern touch. Serve for breakfast with sausages and eggs or as a side dish at dinner.

1 egg, slightly beaten
2 tablespoons milk
3/4 cup cornmeal
3 tablespoons Parmesan cheese
3/4 teaspoon dried Italian seasoning or 1 teaspoon finely chopped fresh basil
1/4 teaspoon salt
1/8 teaspoon freshly ground pepper
3 large green tomatoes, cut into 1/2-inch-thick slices
3 to 4 tablespoons vegetable oil

Combine egg and milk in a shallow bowl. In another shallow bowl, combine cornmeal, Parmesan cheese, Italian seasoning, salt, and pepper. Dip tomato slices into egg mixture, then into cornmeal mixture. Heat oil in a 10-inch skillet over medium heat. Add tomatoes in a single layer. Cook until golden on one side; turn and cook other side. Repeat with remaining tomato slices. Makes about 15 slices.

Sauces & Condiments

The cooperative tomato seems to blend well with almost any food. This is quite evident when it comes to sauces and various types of relishes or uncooked sauces.

With the current interest in grilling, slightly spicy, tart toppings provide a colorful contrast in flavor and texture to fish, poultry, and meats. Best of all, most of the sauces can be made ahead and kept in the refrigerator for several days.

Both fresh and processed tomatoes are handy for versatile tomato sauces. Our Three-Tomato Sauce, made with canned tomato puree and canned diced tomatoes in addition to freshly chopped ones, is handy to have on hand for making pasta or pizza dishes.

Garden Path Salsa

A mild salsa featuring fresh vegetables that complement grilled meats and poultry.

4 plum tomatoes, chopped
2 green onions, chopped
1 small cucumber, peeled, seeded, and chopped
1 mild green chile, seeded and chopped
1 ear corn, cooked and cut off the cob
1/2 teaspoon salt
1 tablespoon chopped cilantro

Combine all ingredients in a medium-size bowl. Cover and refrigerate at least 2 hours or overnight. Makes 3 cups.

Tip

To ripen tomatoes that are not quite ripe, keep them in a moderately warm room until they are ripe.

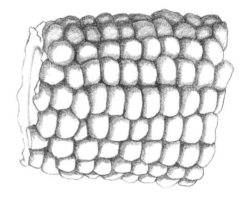

Fresh Salsa Verde

A refreshing relish made with green tomatoes to serve with grilled chicken or roasted pork.

2 medium-size green tomatoes, chopped
1 jalapeño chile, seeded and finely chopped
4 green onions, chopped
2 tablespoons chopped cilantro leaves
1/4 teaspoon salt

Combine all ingredients in a small bowl. Serve at once or cover and refrigerate overnight. Makes 2 1/2 cups.

Variation

For a milder salsa, substitute 1 chopped and seeded mild green chile for the jalapeño.

Black Bean—Tomato Relish

A tasty way to add color and flavor to roasted pork or broiled chicken breasts.

1 (15- to 16-oz.) can black beans, drained and rinsed
2 plum tomatoes, chopped
1 small yellow bell pepper, chopped
2 green onions, chopped
1 fresh mild green chile, seeded and chopped
1 tablespoon vegetable oil
1 tablespoon fresh lime juice or lemon juice
1/4 teaspoon salt

Combine all ingredients in a 1-quart bowl. Cover and refrigerate at least 1 hour or up to 8 hours. Makes 2 1/2 cups.

Home-style Tomato Sauce

If making this uncooked sauce ahead, refrigerate and stir just before serving.

3 large tomatoes, peeled
1 garlic clove
1 tablespoon olive oil or vegetable oil
1 tablespoon chopped chives
1 tablespoon chopped parsley
2 tablespoons sun-dried tomatoes in oil, drained and coarsely chopped
1/2 teaspoon salt
1/8 teaspoon freshly ground pepper

Halve tomatoes crosswise. Gently squeeze out and discard seeds. Place tomato halves in a blender or food processor with garlic, oil, chives, parsley, sun-dried tomatoes, salt, and pepper. Process until pureed. Serve at once or cover and refrigerate up to 2 days, if desired. Spoon over meat loaf, pâté, or terrine. Makes 3 1/3 cups.

Tip

To peel tomatoes, place in boiling water about 45 seconds. Using a slotted spoon, remove tomatoes from boiling water and immediately place in cold water to cool. Tomato skins should slip off easily.

Three-Tomato Sauce

This is a versatile sauce to freeze and keep on hand for last-minute pasta dishes.

1 tablespoon vegetable oil
1 medium-size onion, finely chopped
1 garlic clove, crushed
2 fresh tomatoes, peeled, seeded, and chopped
1 (16-oz.) can diced peeled tomatoes
1 (16-oz.) can tomato puree
1 teaspoon chopped fresh thyme or 1/4 teaspoon dried leaf thyme
1 teaspoon chopped fresh oregano or 1/4 teaspoon dried leaf oregano
2 tablespoons chopped cilantro
2 tablespoons chopped parsley
1/2 teaspoon salt
1/8 teaspoon freshly ground pepper

Heat oil in a 3-quart saucepan. Add onion and garlic; sauté until onion is softened. Stir in remaining ingredients. Bring to a boil; reduce heat and simmer, uncovered, 30 to 35 minutes or until slightly thickened. Spoon over cooked pasta or cool and freeze in airtight containers up to 1 month. Makes about 5 cups.

Chowchow

An old-fashioned relish that is still popular today, this can be used as an appetizing accompaniment to hamburgers as well as chicken and pork dishes.

2 green tomatoes, finely chopped
4 green onions, finely chopped
1 green bell pepper, finely chopped
1 cup shredded cabbage
2 tablespoons salt
3/4 cup white vinegar
3/4 cup sugar
1 teaspoon Dijon mustard
1/2 teaspoon celery seeds
1 tablespoon pickling spices in cheesecloth bag
1/2 teaspoon mustard seeds

Combine tomatoes, onions, bell pepper, and cabbage in a large bowl. Sprinkle with salt; let stand about 3 hours. Drain well in a colander, squeezing out excess moisture. Bring vinegar, sugar, mustard, celery seeds, pickling spices, and mustard seeds to a boil in a nonreactive 2-quart saucepan. Cover and simmer 5 minutes. Add well-drained vegetables; bring to a boil and simmer 5 minutes. Makes 3 cups.

 Tip

This can be spooned into jars and refrigerated up to 1 week.

Sweet-Sour Sauce

Transform leftover pork or poultry into an exciting creation with this easy sauce.

1 (8-oz.) can tomato sauce
1 tablespoon cornstarch
2 tablespoons soy sauce
1/3 cup packed brown sugar
1 green bell pepper, thinly sliced
1 (8-oz.) can crushed pineapple in juice

Combine tomato sauce, cornstarch, and soy sauce in a small saucepan. Add brown sugar, bell pepper, and crushed pineapple with juice. Cook, stirring, over medium heat until thickened. Serve warm. Makes 2 1/3 cups sauce.

Double-Tomato Sauce for Fish

*The addition of tomato paste to the fresh tomatoes gives this sauce
more body and a richer tomato flavor.*

2 tablespoons vegetable oil
1/4 cup chopped onion
2 large tomatoes, peeled, seeded, and chopped
2 tablespoons canned tomato paste
2 teaspoons sugar
1/2 teaspoon salt
1/8 teaspoon freshly ground pepper

Heat oil in a medium-size skillet over medium heat. Add onion; cook about 5 minutes or until onion is softened. Add tomatoes, tomato paste, sugar, salt, and pepper. Simmer 10 minutes, stirring occasionally. Spoon over grilled fish. Makes 1 1/2 cups sauce.

Tip

Leftover tomato paste can be spooned into 1-tablespoon portions and frozen on a waxed paper–lined tray, then removed and placed in a plastic freezer bag. Remove as needed and use frozen.

Marinara Sauce with Fresh Herbs

Make this ahead and refrigerate or freeze to have on hand for pasta dishes.

2 tablespoons vegetable or olive oil
2 medium-size onions, chopped
2 garlic cloves, crushed
2 medium-size carrots, finely chopped
8 medium-size tomatoes, seeded and coarsely chopped
2 tablespoons coarsely chopped fresh basil
2 teaspoons coarsely chopped fresh oregano
2 tablespoons coarsely chopped fresh parsley
1 teaspoon salt
1/4 teaspoon freshly ground pepper

Heat oil in a 3-quart saucepan. Add onions, garlic, and carrots. Sauté 2 or 3 minutes. Stir in tomatoes, basil, oregano, parsley, salt, and pepper. Cover and simmer 20 minutes. Uncover; simmer 10 minutes. Pour into a blender or food processor; process until pureed. Makes about 5 cups sauce.

Tip

If fresh herbs aren't available, substitute about one-third the amount of the dried leaf herb, less of a ground herb.

Seafood Cocktail Sauce

A popular sauce for shrimp or crab appetizers.

1 cup ketchup or chili sauce
1 tablespoon prepared horseradish
2 teaspoons Worcestershire sauce
Several drops hot pepper sauce

Combine all ingredients in a small bowl. Makes about 1 cup sauce.

Homemade Ketchup

When fresh tomatoes are plentiful, make a batch of ketchup.

24 plum tomatoes, seeded and chopped (4 to 4 1/2 lbs.)
2 onions, chopped
1 3/4 cups light corn syrup
1 1/2 teaspoons ground paprika
3/4 cup cider vinegar
1 1/2 teaspoons coarse salt
1 tablespoon whole allspice
1 1/2 teaspoons mustard seeds
3 cinnamon sticks, halved
1 1/2 teaspoons whole cloves

Combine tomatoes, onions, corn syrup, paprika, vinegar, and salt in a 4-quart nonreactive saucepan. Tie allspice, mustard seeds, cinnamon sticks, and cloves in cheesecloth. Add to tomato mixture. Cook, uncovered, stirring occasionally, over medium-low heat about 40 minutes or until desired thickness. Remove spice bag. Pour tomato mixture into a blender or food processor in batches, if necessary. Process until pureed. Pour through a strainer, pressing with back of spoon to remove all solids. Pour into hot sterilized jars and seal. Refrigerate up to 2 weeks. Makes 3 1/2 to 4 cups.

Variation

To keep ketchup longer, pour into hot sterilized pint or half-pint jars, leaving 1/4-inch head space. Cover jars with 2-piece vacuum lids; tighten by hand. Place on a rack in a tall pot. Add enough hot water to cover jars by at least 1 inch over tops. Cover pot; bring water to a boil. Boil 15 minutes. Remove jars; cool at room temperature. Check that all jars have sealed. Store in a cool dry place. Makes 2 pints or 4 half-pints.

 Tip

To remove seeds, first cut the tomato in half crosswise. Then lightly squeeze each half and the seeds will fall out.

Home-style Chili Sauce

Keep this chili sauce on hand to enhance your favorite meats and sandwiches.

5 or 6 medium-size tomatoes, coarsely chopped
1 large onion, chopped
1 red bell pepper, chopped
1/3 cup sugar
1/3 cup light corn syrup
1/2 cup vinegar
1 cinnamon stick
1/2 teaspoon whole cloves
1/2 teaspoon whole allspice
1/2 teaspoon salt

Combine tomatoes, onion, pepper, sugar, corn syrup, and vinegar in a nonreactive 2-quart saucepan. Tie cinnamon stick, cloves, and allspice in cheesecloth; add to tomatoes with salt. Simmer, stirring occasionally, 40 to 50 minutes or until thick. Remove and discard spices. Cover and refrigerate up to 2 weeks. To keep longer, process according to directions on opposite page. Makes about 3 cups.

CANNED TOMATOES

Dip small to medium-size ripe but firm tomatoes in boiling water for 30 to 60 seconds. Immediately place in cold water. Remove skins and cores.

Add 2 tablespoons bottled lemon juice to each quart canning jar or add 1 tablespoon bottled lemon juice to each pint canning jar. Pack whole or halved tomatoes in jars. Add hot water to within 1/2 inch of top of jars. If desired add 1/2 teaspoon noniodized salt to each quart or 1/4 teaspoon salt to each pint jar. Remove air bubbles with a nonmetallic spatula.

Cover jars with two-piece vacuum lids; tighten by hand. Place jars on a rack in a tall pot. Add enough hot water to cover jars by at least 1 inch over tops. Cover; bring to a boil. Boil gently 45 minutes for quarts and 40 minutes for pints. Remove jars. Cool at room temperature for about 12 hours. Check that all jars have sealed. Store in a dark cool dry place.

About three pounds of fresh tomatoes are needed to make one quart of canned tomatoes.

OVEN-DRIED TOMATOES

Place a rack in a 15 × 10-inch shallow baking pan and lightly grease or spray with nonstick coating.

For slices: Cut medium-size or large unpeeled tomatoes into 3/8-inch crosswise slices. Place a single layer on coated rack in pan. Dry, uncovered, in a 200°F (95°C) oven 5 to 7 hours or until slightly pliable, yet dry to the touch.

For halves: Cut medium-size unpeeled plum tomatoes lengthwise into halves. Place in a single layer, cut side up, on coated rack in pan. Dry, uncovered, in a 200°F (95°C) oven 9 to 11 hours or until slightly pliable, yet dry to the touch.

To store: Keep dried slices or halves in airtight containers in the refrigerator. If desired, cover with olive oil or vegetable oil and add your favorite herbs.

Index